I0013256

AI-Powered Content Creation

How AI is Changing Writing, Design, and Music A Guide to AI Tools for Creators, Marketers, and Entrepreneurs

Greyson Chesterfield

COPYRIGHT

DISCLAIMER

The information provided in this book is for general informational purposes only. All content in this book reflects the author's views and is based on their research, knowledge, and experiences. The author and publisher make no representations or warranties of any kind concerning the completeness, accuracy, reliability, suitability, or availability of the information contained herein.

This book is not intended to be a substitute for professional advice, diagnosis, or treatment. Readers should seek professional advice for any specific concerns or conditions. The author and publisher disclaim any liability or responsibility for any direct, indirect, incidental, or consequential loss or damage arising from the use of the information contained in this book.

Chapter 1: Getting Started with AI in Content Creation

Summary

Artificial Intelligence (AI) is no longer a futuristic concept—it is already reshaping how we approach content creation in writing, design, and music. If you're a creator, marketer, or entrepreneur, AI is not something to overlook; it's the tool you need to work smarter, faster, and more efficiently. In this chapter, we will dive deep into what AI is, explore how it's transforming creative fields, and help you understand how you can leverage AI to enhance your own projects.

We'll also give you a glimpse into how this book is structured, what tools you'll learn about, and how each chapter builds on the last to empower you with practical AI skills that you can immediately apply to your creative work.

Introduction to AI and How It's Changing Writing, Design, and Music

AI is revolutionizing content creation by automating time-consuming tasks, providing new ways to enhance creativity, and even generating new content entirely. At its core, AI is the simulation of human intelligence processes by machines—whether it's learning from data, recognizing patterns, or generating new outputs based on input. Think of AI as your creative assistant—one that never tires, can work at lightning speed, and can offer suggestions or produce content at the click of a button.

AI is already making waves across various industries, and the creative fields of writing, design, and music are no exception. From drafting blog posts and marketing copy to generating design ideas and composing original music, AI is helping creators produce high-quality work quickly and efficiently. The potential for AI to revolutionize content creation is limitless.

In Writing

AI tools like GPT-3 (the model behind ChatGPT) are designed to understand language and generate coherent text based on a prompt. This means that writers can use AI for brainstorming ideas, drafting articles, refining content, and even creating entire blog posts or marketing copy without starting from scratch. These tools are trained on vast datasets, enabling them to mimic different writing styles, tones, and structures. They offer writers the opportunity to focus on higher-level creative tasks while AI handles the grunt work of writing.

In Design

AI in design isn't just about making things look pretty. It's about making the design process more efficient and helping designers explore new possibilities faster. Tools like Canva's AI-powered design suggestions or Adobe Sensei use machine learning to automate design tasks, recommend layouts, and even create logos based on inputted guidelines. These tools help both beginner and professional designers alike, speeding up workflows and allowing them to experiment with creative ideas quickly.

In Music

AI is also changing the music industry by assisting musicians and producers in composing music, generating melodies, and even mixing tracks. AI tools like Amper Music, AIVA, and OpenAI's MuseNet can analyze existing music and generate original compositions in various genres. These tools can be a game-changer for musicians who may not have formal training in music theory, enabling them to create professional-sounding tracks with minimal technical knowledge.

By the end of this chapter, you'll see how AI is enhancing these creative processes and why it's important for creators to embrace AI as a vital tool in their toolkit.

What AI Is and How It Can Help You Create Content Faster and Smarter

AI is often misunderstood. Some think of it as a robot-like entity, but at its core, AI is simply a collection of algorithms that allow machines to perform tasks that typically require human intelligence. In the context of content creation, AI can:

1. **Automate Repetitive Tasks:** AI can take over tedious, repetitive tasks like proofreading, resizing images, or suggesting design elements. This saves creators valuable time to focus on more strategic and creative decisions.

2. **Generate Content:** AI can write articles, compose music, and create design templates by processing large amounts of data and identifying patterns. It can suggest starting points, help with brainstorming, or even generate full drafts for you to refine.

3. **Enhance Creativity:** AI is a powerful tool for generating new ideas, patterns, and possibilities that you may not have considered. It can act as a creative partner, offering suggestions, ideas, and alternatives that push the boundaries of your imagination.

4. **Improve Decision Making:** AI tools can provide data-driven insights into trends, performance, and audience preferences. For marketers and

entrepreneurs, AI can help tailor content and strategies based on what resonates with your target audience.

By using AI in your content creation process, you can work more efficiently, reduce time spent on low-value tasks, and enhance the quality of your creative output. In short, AI helps you create smarter, faster, and with more innovation.

Overview of the Book and What You Will Learn

This book will guide you step-by-step through the world of AI-powered content creation. We'll explore how AI tools work, how to integrate them into your existing workflows, and how to use them to elevate your content in writing, design, and music.

In the coming chapters, you'll:

- **Learn about the different types of AI tools** that are transforming creative processes in writing, design, and music.

- **Experiment with hands-on projects** that walk you through practical use cases, from generating blog posts to designing logos and composing music with AI.

- **Understand the future of AI in content creation** and how to stay ahead of the curve by adopting emerging AI technologies.

- **Explore real-world applications** with case studies and examples of AI being used by creators, marketers, and entrepreneurs in various industries.

By the end of this book, you'll be able to confidently integrate AI tools into your daily creative practices. Whether you're a marketer looking to produce high-quality content at scale, a writer seeking inspiration, a designer exploring new creative directions, or a musician composing original tracks, AI will be your ultimate tool for increasing productivity and enhancing creativity.

Real-World Applications

AI tools are not just theoretical concepts—they are already having a profound impact on the way creators, marketers, and entrepreneurs work. Here are some practical ways AI is being used in the real world:

For Marketers

Marketers are using AI to generate content quickly and at scale. Tools like Jasper (formerly Jarvis) and Copy.ai can write product descriptions, social media posts, and even email campaigns, saving marketers hours of manual work. AI can also help optimize content based on data, ensuring that what you create resonates with your audience.

- **Example**: A digital marketing agency uses AI to generate blog posts and social media content in half the time, allowing them to scale their operations and serve more clients.

For Writers

AI tools are helping writers with brainstorming ideas, drafting articles, and even editing. Writers can input topics, and the AI will generate an outline or a first draft to work from. AI is also used in grammar and style checkers like Grammarly, which helps ensure content is polished and error-free.

- **Example**: An author uses AI to generate character ideas and plot outlines, which sparks inspiration for their next novel.

For Entrepreneurs

Entrepreneurs can use AI tools for everything from creating logos and brand materials to writing sales copy and generating emails. By using AI to automate these tasks, entrepreneurs can focus more on strategy and scaling their businesses.

- **Example**: A startup entrepreneur uses an AI tool to design their brand identity, create marketing copy, and generate social media posts, all while saving valuable time.

How AI Can Help Marketers, Writers, and Entrepreneurs

No matter your profession, AI can dramatically improve how you create content. Whether you're producing marketing materials, writing blog posts, designing visuals, or composing music, AI is a tool that can help you streamline your process, cut down on repetitive tasks, and boost creativity.

- **For Marketers**: AI can help marketers generate personalized emails, advertisements, and landing pages at scale. AI-based analytics tools can also help you track the performance of your content, offering insights that allow you to adjust strategies quickly.

- **For Writers**: Writers can use AI to automate the writing process, receive feedback on their work, and refine their style and structure. AI-powered writing assistants can help writers overcome writer's block and ensure content quality and consistency.

- **For Entrepreneurs**: Entrepreneurs can use AI to enhance branding efforts, create effective content strategies, and increase operational efficiency. With AI's ability to predict trends and optimize workflows, entrepreneurs can focus on growing their business and expanding their reach.

Ways to Start Using AI in Your Own Work

If you're ready to dive in and start using AI tools in your own work, here's how you can begin:

1. **Identify Tasks You Can Automate**: Start by looking at your daily tasks and identifying areas where AI can save you time. This might include automating repetitive tasks like writing basic copy, generating images, or composing music.

2. **Experiment with Free AI Tools**: There are many free and accessible AI tools available to get you started. Try out tools like ChatGPT for writing, Canva for design, or Soundraw for music. Experiment with these tools to see how they fit into your creative process.

3. **Start Small, Then Scale Up**: Begin by using AI for small tasks and gradually scale up as you become more comfortable. Once you understand the tool's potential, integrate it into larger projects.

4. **Embrace Iteration**: AI tools work best when used iteratively. Start with a basic draft or idea,

let the AI generate a starting point, and then refine and expand upon it yourself.

By taking small steps to integrate AI into your creative work, you can begin reaping the benefits of enhanced productivity, improved creativity, and higher-quality content.

Chapter 2: AI Basics—How It Works

Summary

Artificial Intelligence (AI) isn't just some buzzword anymore—it's a fundamental technology that is already shaping the future of content creation, from writing and design to music and marketing. In this chapter, we're going to break down key AI concepts in a simple way, without getting too deep into technical jargon, so you can understand how it works and why it matters to you.

By the end of this chapter, you'll have a clearer idea of how AI differs from traditional software, how it's designed to learn and improve over time, and how it powers the tools you're going to use throughout this book. Whether you're a writer, designer, or entrepreneur, understanding the basics of AI will give you the foundation to start harnessing its full potential in your creative work.

Introduction to Key AI Terms Like Machine Learning and Neural Networks in Simple Language

Let's begin by demystifying some of the most common AI-related terms that you're likely to encounter in this book.

What is AI?

Artificial Intelligence is the field of computer science focused on creating machines and software that can mimic human intelligence. These machines can understand data, learn from it, make decisions, and improve over time. Unlike traditional software that operates based on specific instructions, AI systems learn from data and adapt to new situations.

In simpler terms, AI is like giving a machine the ability to think, learn, and make decisions—just like we do. The difference is that machines do this much faster and can handle vast amounts of data that we could never process on our own.

Machine Learning (ML)

Machine Learning is a subset of AI that focuses on training machines to recognize patterns in data and make predictions based on those patterns. The more data you feed into an ML model, the better it becomes at making accurate predictions or decisions.

Think of machine learning as teaching a system to improve itself over time based on experience—without explicitly programming it to do so. For example, if you give an AI tool like a writing assistant thousands of examples of well-written content, it will learn what constitutes "good" writing and use that knowledge to generate new content.

- **Example**: You might use a recommendation system on Netflix. The more you watch and rate shows, the better the system gets at recommending what you might enjoy. This is powered by machine learning.

Neural Networks

Neural Networks are a core component of many AI systems, especially those used in machine learning and deep learning. Inspired by how the human brain works, a neural network is made up of layers of nodes (also called neurons) that process data and pass information to each other.

Neural networks are used to recognize patterns in data, like identifying faces in photos, translating languages, or generating realistic-sounding speech. These networks can "learn" to improve their predictions by adjusting the connections between neurons as they process more data. In essence, neural networks are designed to mimic human cognitive functions like vision, speech, and reasoning.

- **Example**: Think of a neural network as a series of decision-making steps, where each step gets you closer to an answer. For instance, when an AI generates an image based on a description, each neural layer helps improve the output until the final result is a polished image.

Deep Learning

Deep Learning is a specific type of machine learning that uses large neural networks with many layers to process data. Deep learning is particularly powerful for tasks that involve large amounts of unstructured data, such as images, speech, and text.

While machine learning can work with relatively simple models, deep learning requires massive datasets and powerful computing resources. This is why deep learning is used in tasks like generating realistic images, translating text, or even composing music.

- **Example**: When you upload a photo to Instagram and it automatically tags your friends, that's deep learning at work. The AI system has learned to recognize faces in your photos based on patterns in its vast dataset.

Natural Language Processing (NLP)

Natural Language Processing (NLP) is another critical field within AI that focuses on enabling machines to understand and process human language. Whether it's text or speech, NLP tools allow computers to interpret, generate, and respond to language in ways that feel natural to humans.

In the context of writing, NLP models like GPT-3 (used in tools like ChatGPT) are trained on enormous amounts of text data, learning grammar, syntax, and even context, so they can generate text that sounds coherent and natural.

- **Example**: When you ask your phone to send a text, it uses NLP to understand what you want and convert your spoken words into written text.

How AI Works and What Makes It Different from Regular Software

Now that we have an understanding of the core terms, let's take a deeper look at how AI actually works and what makes it different from traditional software.

Traditional Software vs. AI

Traditional software is like following a recipe—each step is clearly defined, and the system will do exactly what it's told. For example, a calculator will always add, subtract, multiply, or divide numbers based on the instructions it receives. You give it a number, it performs a fixed operation, and you get a result.

AI, on the other hand, is more like a flexible, self-improving system. Instead of strictly following a set of programmed instructions, AI systems learn from data and adapt over time. They can make decisions, predict outcomes, and even generate new content based on patterns they've identified in the data.

For example, traditional software might sort a list of numbers in ascending order based on the exact instructions given, while an AI system might look for patterns in the data and suggest ways to organize it in a way that maximizes efficiency or insights.

Training vs. Programming

In traditional software development, programmers write code to tell the system exactly what to do. AI, however, uses training data to "learn" how to make decisions. It's like teaching a child how to recognize animals by showing them thousands of pictures of cats, dogs, and birds.

In AI training, the more data you provide, the better the system gets at predicting or making decisions. This is the essence of machine learning and neural networks. The system doesn't rely on fixed instructions but rather learns from examples and improves itself as it processes more data.

- **Example**: If you train an AI tool on thousands of design examples, it can learn to create new, similar designs that match the style and preferences it's been trained on.

Why AI Isn't Just Another Software Tool

The key difference between AI and traditional software is the concept of autonomy and learning. AI is designed to evolve and improve as it processes more information. It can handle ambiguous situations, process vast amounts of unstructured data (like text or images), and even generate new content.

Traditional software, by contrast, follows fixed rules and instructions. It can't adapt or learn on its own unless it's explicitly programmed to do so. AI can make decisions, predict outcomes, and create new content without human intervention, provided it's given the right kind of data and training.

Learning Objectives

By the end of this chapter, you should be able to:

1. **Understand the Basics of AI (Without the Tech Jargon)**: You'll know what AI is, how it works, and why it's different from traditional software. This will give you a solid foundation to understand AI tools in the coming chapters.

2. **Understand What AI Tools Do and How They Can Help You**: You'll understand how AI tools—whether for writing, design, or music—are powered by machine learning and neural networks. This will help you grasp how these tools make decisions, generate content, and improve over time.

Hands-On Activity

In this section, we'll introduce you to some simple AI tools that will help you apply what you've learned so far. The goal here is to familiarize you with how AI responds to different instructions, as this will lay the groundwork for later hands-on projects.

Explore AI: Try Using an AI Tool for Writing or Design and See How It Responds to Different Instructions

Take some time to experiment with an AI-powered tool of your choice. If you're a writer, try using a text generator like ChatGPT. If you're a designer, try a tool like Canva's AI-powered design suggestions. Here's what to do:

1. **Choose Your Tool**: For writing, try generating a paragraph or short blog post with ChatGPT. For

design, choose a template on Canva and let the AI make suggestions.

2. **Input a Simple Prompt**: For ChatGPT, try something like: "Write a 200-word blog post on the benefits of using AI for creativity." For Canva, try customizing a design by selecting a theme and letting AI choose complementary elements.

3. **Observe the Output**: Look at the content or design suggestions generated by the AI. How well did it understand your request? How close is it to what you had in mind?

Compare Outputs: Compare AI-Made Content with Human-Made Content

Now, compare the output generated by the AI with something you or a human creator has made. Here are some questions to reflect on:

- How well did the AI understand the prompt or design guidelines?

- Did the AI output meet your expectations in terms of quality and relevance?

- How does the AI-generated content compare with human-made content in terms of creativity, tone, and style?

Reflection: After completing this exercise, reflect on how AI's ability to process large amounts of data allows it to generate ideas, designs, and text based on patterns it has learned. Consider how this might enhance your own creative process.

Real-World Applications

AI is not just theoretical—it's being used in creative industries right now to speed up workflows, improve content quality, and provide new creative possibilities. Let's look at how AI is being used in real-world applications:

Speeding Up Creative Tasks

In writing, AI tools like ChatGPT can quickly generate drafts, outlines, or ideas, saving writers hours of time. In design, AI tools like Canva or Adobe Sensei can automatically suggest layouts, color schemes, and typography based on your preferences. This allows creatives to spend more time refining and improving their work rather than starting from scratch.

Making Decisions Based on Data

AI tools can also help marketers and entrepreneurs make data-driven decisions. By analyzing large amounts of data, AI tools can generate insights into customer behavior, preferences, and trends. For example, an AI tool might help a marketer generate content that resonates with a specific target audience based on data it has collected.

Enhancing Creativity

AI can push the boundaries of creativity by suggesting new ideas, generating content, and even creating new forms of art. Whether it's generating music, designing visuals, or writing stories, AI can inspire new possibilities and open up creative pathways that might not have been considered otherwise.

Chapter 3: AI in Writing—From Drafting to Polishing

Summary

Artificial Intelligence is rapidly transforming the writing process, taking it from the traditional model of pen-on-paper (or fingers-on-keyboard) to an intelligent, data-driven, and highly efficient creative tool. What was once a labor-intensive task for writers, bloggers, marketers, and authors is now augmented with AI tools that can help with everything from brainstorming ideas to final polishing of a manuscript or marketing copy. In this chapter, we will take a deep dive into how AI is revolutionizing the writing, editing, and content strategy landscape. We'll look at various tools—from GPT-based text generation platforms to grammar checkers and summarizers—and how they can optimize your writing process.

Whether you're a seasoned writer, a marketing professional, or a content creator, AI has proven its worth in the world of writing. This chapter is designed to help you understand how AI can be integrated into your writing workflow, improve your productivity, and keep you focused on the parts of writing that require true human creativity. We will also cover the ethical considerations surrounding AI writing tools, such as plagiarism and originality, so you can confidently use AI without compromising your integrity.

The Role of AI in Writing

How AI Enhances the Writing Process

Writing is a creative endeavor that involves not only creativity but also a great deal of time and effort. The process of developing ideas, structuring content, writing drafts, revising, and finalizing a piece can be tedious and time-consuming, especially when you're juggling multiple writing tasks at once. AI tools are stepping in to streamline this process, offering assistance in every phase—from brainstorming ideas to editing and finalizing drafts.

One of the most significant ways AI enhances writing is by automating repetitive tasks, reducing cognitive load, and offering suggestions based on data-driven analysis. AI-powered tools allow you to focus on higher-level creative tasks like strategy, storytelling, and tone, while the AI handles the mechanics of writing—grammar, spelling, and even the initial drafts.

Types of AI Tools for Writing

1. **Text Generation**: Tools like OpenAI's GPT-3, Jasper, and Copy.ai are capable of generating high-quality text from a simple prompt. Whether you're looking to create an entire blog post, marketing copy, or even a short story, AI can generate text that serves as the first draft, saving you significant time.

2. **Grammar and Style Checkers**: Tools like Grammarly, Hemingway Editor, and ProWritingAid help improve the clarity, flow, and grammar of your writing. They are essential for ensuring your writing is error-free and stylistically sound.

3. **Summarization Tools**: AI tools can summarize large bodies of text, helping you quickly distill complex documents or articles into key points. This is particularly useful for researchers, journalists, and content creators who need to stay on top of large amounts of information.

4. **Idea Generation and Outlining Tools**: AI can help you brainstorm new ideas, suggest keywords, or even generate outlines based on a specific topic or keyword. These tools are incredibly useful for overcoming writer's block and structuring your thoughts efficiently.

5. **Personalized Writing Assistants**: As you use AI more frequently, some AI tools will adapt to your writing style, providing customized feedback, suggestions, and writing prompts. This makes it easier for you to maintain consistency across various pieces of content.

Learning Objectives

By the end of this chapter, you will:

1. **Master AI Writing Tools**: You'll understand the best practices for using AI writing tools

effectively, ensuring that they work for you rather than becoming a hindrance.

2. **Use AI for Brainstorming and Outlining**: Learn how to prompt AI tools to generate creative ideas and solid outlines for articles, blog posts, or marketing content.

3. **Polish Your Writing with AI**: Discover how to use AI-based grammar and style checkers to refine your writing, ensuring that it's polished and professional.

4. **Understand Ethical Considerations**: Learn the ethical implications of using AI in writing, including concerns about plagiarism, originality, and maintaining authenticity.

Best Practices for Prompting AI Writing Tools Effectively

AI-powered writing tools are incredibly powerful, but they only work well if you know how to communicate with them. The key to using these tools effectively is mastering the art of prompting. AI writing models, especially large language models like GPT-3, are capable of understanding and responding to a wide range of inputs, but the quality of the output heavily depends on the clarity and specificity of your prompts.

Creating Clear, Detailed Prompts

1. **Be Specific**: Instead of asking for a vague request like "Write an article about AI," provide more specific details. For example: "Write a 500-word blog post that explains the impact of AI on content creation in the marketing industry, focusing on time-saving benefits for marketers."

2. **Define the Structure**: If you're looking for a certain type of content, such as a list or a how-to guide, specify that in the prompt. Example: "Generate a step-by-step guide for creating social media ad copy using AI."

3. **Incorporate Tone and Style**: If you want the writing to follow a certain tone (formal, conversational, humorous, etc.), specify that in your prompt. Example: "Write a casual blog post about AI for content creators in a friendly and engaging tone."

4. **Iterate and Refine**: AI doesn't always get it right on the first try, so don't be afraid to refine your prompt or ask the AI to revise its response. For instance, you might ask, "Can you rewrite this introduction in a more engaging tone?" or "Expand on the benefits of using AI in content marketing."

By experimenting with different types of prompts, you'll learn what works best for your writing style and what the AI is capable of producing.

Using AI for Brainstorming, Outlining, and Drafting

AI can be a valuable tool for the early stages of writing. It can help you overcome writer's block, generate new ideas, and quickly create outlines. Here's how you can use AI effectively in these stages:

Brainstorming Ideas

Sometimes the hardest part of writing is coming up with the ideas in the first place. AI tools are great for sparking new concepts and brainstorming potential topics.

- **Example**: Ask an AI tool, "What are some trending topics for a blog post on digital marketing?" The AI can provide a list of relevant topics, giving you a starting point for your content creation process.

Creating Outlines

Once you have a topic in mind, you can use AI to generate an outline for your article, blog post, or marketing content.

- **Example**: You might prompt an AI with: "Create an outline for a blog post on how AI can improve customer service in the retail industry." The AI might generate an outline that looks like this:

  1. Introduction: Why AI is revolutionizing customer service

  2. Key Benefits of AI in Customer Service

  3. Real-world Examples of AI in Retail

  4. Challenges and Considerations

  5. Conclusion: Future Trends

With this outline in hand, you can move on to drafting the content, confident that the structure is solid.

Drafting Content

Using AI to generate a first draft is one of the most time-saving aspects of AI-assisted writing. The AI can take your outline and flesh it out into a full article, blog post, or social media content.

- **Example**: Once you've got your outline, you can input it into the AI tool and ask it to "expand the outline into a full blog post." The AI will generate text for each section of the outline, and you can refine it further from there.

Polishing Your Writing with AI Tools

Once you've got your draft in place, AI tools can help you refine and polish your writing to ensure it's clear, professional, and error-free. Here are a few ways AI can help with editing and polishing:

Grammar and Spelling Check

Tools like Grammarly and ProWritingAid are invaluable when it comes to identifying and correcting spelling, grammar, and punctuation errors. These tools don't just flag mistakes—they also provide suggestions for improving sentence structure and style.

- **Example**: After generating an article, you can run it through a grammar checker to catch any spelling mistakes, improper punctuation, or awkward phrasing. The AI will suggest corrections and alternatives, which you can accept or revise as necessary.

Style and Clarity Improvement

Beyond grammar, AI tools can help you improve the overall style and clarity of your writing. Hemingway Editor, for instance, focuses on making your writing more concise, direct, and easier to read.

- **Example**: If your article feels overly complicated or dense, you can run it through Hemingway Editor, which will highlight areas where you can simplify the language, shorten sentences, and improve readability.

Plagiarism Detection

It's essential to ensure that your content is original, especially when using AI to generate text. Plagiarism checkers like Copyscape or Turnitin are great for making sure your writing is unique and hasn't inadvertently copied from other sources.

- **Example**: After generating content with AI, you can run it through a plagiarism checker to ensure that the content is free of duplication.

Ethical Considerations: Plagiarism, Originality, and Authenticity

AI writing tools are powerful, but they come with a responsibility to use them ethically. It's essential to maintain originality and authenticity when using AI-generated content. Here's how you can ensure you're using AI ethically:

Avoiding Plagiarism

While AI tools generate content based on patterns they've learned from existing data, they don't intentionally plagiarize. However, AI-generated content might closely resemble existing text if you're not careful. Always run your content through plagiarism detection tools and make sure it's unique.

Maintaining Originality

AI can help you brainstorm, draft, and edit, but the final piece should still reflect your own voice and creativity. Make sure to put your own spin on AI-generated content, adding insights, personality, and perspective that only you can provide.

Transparency

If you're using AI to generate content for clients, readers, or customers, it's essential to be transparent about your use of AI tools. Being upfront about AI-assisted writing fosters trust and ensures you maintain professional integrity.

Practical Applications for AI in Writing

AI tools have a wide range of applications in writing, from crafting marketing copy to drafting long-form blog posts. Here are a few ways different types of writers can benefit from AI:

Marketers Creating Ad Copy or Social Media Content

For marketers, AI tools can help quickly generate attention-grabbing headlines, social media posts, and product descriptions. AI's ability to produce content at scale is invaluable when you're trying to stay on top of ever-changing trends and consumer interests.

Writers Drafting and Editing Blog Posts or Articles

For bloggers or content creators, AI tools like GPT-3 can generate ideas, outlines, and first drafts, while grammar checkers and style editors help ensure the content is polished and error-free. AI can also help writers improve productivity by minimizing the time spent on revisions.

Student/Academic Use

AI writing tools can help students outline research papers, generate ideas, and even draft essays. However, students should use these tools ethically, ensuring they maintain academic integrity and avoid plagiarism by properly citing any AI-generated content.

Chapter 4: Hands-On Project— Building Your First AI-Assisted Writing Workflow

Summary

Artificial Intelligence can be a game-changer for writers, marketers, content creators, and anyone in need of producing quality content quickly and efficiently. However, successfully integrating AI into your writing workflow requires more than just using a tool to generate text. It's about knowing how to combine AI-generated content with your own unique voice, ensuring that the final product resonates with your audience while maintaining a high standard of quality.

In this chapter, we'll guide you through the process of building your very first AI-assisted writing workflow, step by step. We'll use an actual project—writing a blog post or a press release—as a practical example. From gathering initial research to refining your final piece, this chapter will teach you how to maximize the power of AI tools while still maintaining full creative control.

By the end of this chapter, you will have a robust, repeatable AI-assisted writing process that helps you create polished, high-quality content in a fraction of the time.

Learning Objectives

In this chapter, you will:

1. **Gain Practical Skills in Combining AI Text Generation with Manual Editing**
   Learn how to use AI tools to generate content, then manually refine that content to match your

personal voice, style, and messaging goals. AI will serve as your assistant, not a replacement.

2. **Learn How to Iterate and Refine AI-Generated Content for Your Unique Voice**
   Understand how to iterate on AI-generated text to infuse it with your own creativity and ensure it aligns with your brand voice.

3. **Create a Polished Piece of Content from Start to Finish Using AI Assistance**
   From research to final polish, you'll understand how to build a complete workflow that integrates AI-generated drafts into your writing process.

Project Setup: Choose a Topic and Gather Initial Research

1. Selecting a Topic

The first step in building your AI-assisted writing workflow is to choose a topic. Whether you're writing a blog post, a press release, an article, or any other piece of content, selecting a topic that aligns with your audience's interests is key. AI tools can help generate ideas, but it's important to ensure that your topic is relevant to your audience and purpose.

Here are some guidelines for selecting a topic:

- **Consider Your Audience**: What does your target audience care about? If you're writing for an audience in the tech industry, for example, you might choose a topic related to the latest trends in artificial intelligence or software development.

- **Check for Trends**: Use tools like Google Trends or BuzzSumo to find out what topics are currently trending in your niche or industry. AI can help you create content that's aligned with the current conversation.

- **Use AI for Idea Generation**: If you're stuck, don't hesitate to use AI to help you brainstorm. Tools like ChatGPT can generate ideas based on prompts like, "What are the latest topics in digital marketing?" or "What should I write about in a blog post on sustainable living?"

2. Gathering Initial Research

Once you've selected your topic, it's time to gather research. AI can help streamline this process too.

Instead of combing through endless pages of search results, you can use AI-powered summarization tools to pull out key insights from articles, research papers, or books.

Here's how to gather research for your project:

- **Search for Reliable Sources**: Use search engines like Google Scholar, PubMed (for health-related topics), or industry-specific websites to gather reliable research.

- **Use Summarization Tools**: Tools like SMMRY or Resoomer can automatically summarize long articles into key points, helping you quickly gather essential information.

- **Feed Research Into AI**: Once you've gathered research, you can input the key points into your AI writing tool. For example, if you're writing about the role of AI in content creation, you can ask the AI, "Summarize the benefits of AI in content marketing based on recent research."

3. Define Your Content's Structure

Before jumping into writing, it's essential to define the structure of your content. AI tools can help you generate an outline based on the topic you've selected. By inputting basic instructions, you can receive a structured outline that saves you time during the drafting process.

For example, you can input the prompt: "Create a blog post outline on the topic of AI in digital marketing. Include an introduction, benefits of AI, challenges, and future trends."

This outline can be refined and expanded as needed, giving you a framework to work from.

AI Assistance: Use an Online AI Writing Tool to Generate an Outline, First Draft, or Introduction

Now that you have your topic, research, and structure in place, it's time to let the AI assist you in generating the first draft. Here are the specific steps to follow to get the most out of AI tools:

1. Generate the Outline with AI

If you've already created a rough outline, the next step is to ask the AI to expand on it. You can input an outline and ask the AI to generate a more detailed structure or expand on specific points. For example:

- **Prompt to AI**: "Expand on this outline by providing more detail under each heading. Focus on explaining the benefits of AI in marketing and provide real-world examples."

The AI will generate a detailed version of your outline, offering ideas, sub-points, and examples that you can incorporate into your final piece.

2. Generate the First Draft

Once you have your outline, you can input it into your AI tool to generate the first draft of the content. You might provide an instruction like:

- **Prompt to AI**: "Write the introduction of the blog post about AI in digital marketing. Focus on explaining how AI is transforming the way companies interact with customers."

The AI will generate a coherent introduction based on the outline and your prompt. This draft will not be perfect, but it will serve as a strong starting point.

3. Generate Subsequent Sections

Repeat this process for each section of your content. You'll want to generate AI responses for the main points in your outline—benefits, challenges, trends, etc. Remember, AI can create content quickly, but you will need to refine it to ensure it matches your tone and style.

Refinement: Manually Edit for Clarity, Style, and Tone

After you have your AI-generated draft, it's time to refine it. AI tools can generate useful, high-quality content, but human creativity, voice, and clarity are essential to ensuring the piece aligns with your goals and brand guidelines.

1. Review for Coherence and Structure

AI is excellent at generating content quickly, but it may not always flow as naturally as you would like. As you review the draft, ensure the sections are logically ordered, and the content flows from one paragraph to the next. You may need to adjust the transitions between paragraphs and refine the writing to make sure it reads smoothly.

- **Tip**: Focus on maintaining consistency in tone and structure throughout the piece. If the AI shifts in style or tone at any point, adjust it manually to ensure consistency.

2. Refine the Style and Voice

AI tools can generate text quickly, but they might not always align with your personal or brand voice. This is where your creativity comes in. Take time to infuse the AI-generated content with your unique voice, ensuring that the tone matches the intended audience.

- **Tip**: If you're writing for a professional audience, refine the language to ensure it's formal, precise, and authoritative. If you're writing for a casual audience, feel free to add a conversational tone to the text.

3. Improve Clarity and Precision

AI can sometimes generate vague or overly complex sentences. Review each section and refine the language for clarity and precision. Break down overly complex ideas into simpler, more digestible sentences, and remove any unnecessary jargon that might confuse your readers.

- **Tip**: Use grammar and style checkers (like Grammarly or Hemingway Editor) to spot areas where the writing can be simplified or improved for readability.

4. Check for SEO Optimization (If Applicable)

If you're writing for a website, blog, or marketing content, SEO optimization is crucial. Ensure that the AI-generated content contains relevant keywords for SEO and follows best practices for web content (e.g., headings, subheadings, meta descriptions).

- **Tip**: Use tools like Yoast or SEMrush to help with SEO optimization and to ensure your content ranks well on search engines.

Practical Applications

Let's take a closer look at how this process can be applied in different writing scenarios to help you produce content faster while maintaining high quality.

1. Marketers Creating Ad Copy or Social Media Content

AI tools can help marketers generate ad copy or social media content in seconds. For instance, if you need a catchy headline or a social media post, AI tools like Copy.ai or Jasper can generate multiple options based on a simple prompt.

- **Example**: You might prompt the AI, "Generate 5 variations of a Facebook ad copy for a product launch, targeting young professionals interested in sustainable living."

AI can quickly provide you with multiple ad copy options, which you can then refine to match your brand voice and goals.

2. Writers Drafting and Editing Blog Posts or Articles

Bloggers and content writers can use AI for idea generation, outlining, and drafting. Once you have your AI-generated draft, you can edit for tone, style, and clarity, ensuring the final piece reflects your voice.

- **Example**: After the AI generates an introduction and a few key sections of your article, you can iterate on the content to add your personal touch or unique insights.

3. Students/Academics

AI writing tools can be especially helpful for students, enabling them to quickly outline essays, research papers, or reports. However, it's important to follow ethical guidelines and ensure that all AI-generated content is properly cited and does not violate academic integrity.

- **Example**: A student might use an AI tool to generate a draft of a research paper based on a specific topic, but will need to manually refine the content, add citations, and ensure originality.

Conclusion

By now, you should have a solid understanding of how to build an AI-assisted writing workflow. The steps of gathering research, generating outlines, drafting content with AI assistance, and then refining that content are all part of a streamlined, efficient writing process that can help you produce high-quality content quickly.

Remember, while AI can assist with generating content and refining your writing, it's your creativity, voice, and unique perspective that ultimately make the content stand out. By combining the efficiency of AI with your own expertise and originality, you can create compelling, polished content that resonates with your audience.

Chapter 5: AI in Music— Composing Tracks with AI

Summary

Artificial Intelligence has been making significant strides in almost every creative domain, and music is no exception. While AI-generated music might have once seemed like the domain of futuristic sci-fi movies, today, it's a powerful and accessible tool that is transforming the way music is created. AI tools can now assist with everything from composing melodies to mixing and mastering tracks, enabling musicians, podcasters, and content creators to produce high-quality music in a fraction of the time it would take through traditional methods.

In this chapter, we will explore how AI is reshaping music creation, from basic melodies to full tracks. You'll learn how AI tools are being used for composing background music, jingles, soundtracks, and even more complex compositions. Whether you are a beginner with no musical training or an experienced musician looking for a creative boost, this chapter will introduce you to AI music composition tools that can help you create music in new and innovative ways.

Learning Objectives

By the end of this chapter, you will:

1. **Understand How AI Can Assist in Music Composition**:
   Learn how AI can generate music based on input you provide, helping you overcome creative blocks, experiment with new styles, and accelerate the music creation process.

2. **Master AI Tools for Music Creation**:
   Discover how AI tools can be used to compose melodies, build harmonies, create beats, and even produce full tracks. Even without formal

musical training, you'll be able to produce high-quality compositions.

3. **Learn How to Use AI for Mixing and Mastering**:
   Understand how AI can assist with mixing and mastering your tracks to achieve professional sound quality, ensuring your music is ready for release.

4. **Apply AI in Real-World Music Creation**:
   Gain hands-on experience with AI tools and see how they can be applied in real-world scenarios like producing background music for videos, jingles for commercials, or music for podcasts and content creators.

Introduction to AI in Music Creation

AI in music creation is an exciting intersection of technology and creativity. The idea of using machines to compose music is not new, but with the advancements in machine learning and neural networks, AI music tools have evolved significantly in recent years. AI can now generate original melodies, harmonies, and even full arrangements, while also assisting with the production and mixing of tracks.

In the past, creating music required a deep understanding of musical theory, composition, and sometimes expensive studio equipment. Today, AI tools have lowered the barrier to entry for music creation, enabling anyone—from aspiring musicians to content creators—to produce music quickly, professionally, and at scale.

How Does AI Music Creation Work?

AI-generated music works by training algorithms on large datasets of existing music. These algorithms learn patterns in musical composition, such as melody, rhythm, harmony, and structure. Once trained, the AI can generate new compositions by synthesizing those learned patterns into something original.

There are different types of AI models used in music creation, including:

1. **Generative Models**: These models can create completely new music by analyzing patterns in existing works. They can generate melodies,

rhythms, and even full arrangements based on the style of the training data.

2. **Recurrent Neural Networks (RNNs)**: These are used in music to predict the next note in a sequence based on previous notes. RNNs have been successful in producing short compositions, and more recently, they have been applied to longer, more complex musical structures.

3. **Markov Chains**: These statistical models are used to generate music by selecting the next note based on probabilities learned from the existing data. Markov models are less complex than neural networks but still effective for generating simple melodies and harmonies.

4. **Autoencoders and GANs (Generative Adversarial Networks)**: These deep learning models help create high-quality music by learning the distribution of musical elements and generating new compositions that closely resemble the style or genre of the training set.

AI Tools for Music Creation

Several AI tools are currently available for music creators, whether you want to compose background music, create soundtracks for videos, or even produce full songs. These tools use machine learning to generate music based on the user's input, allowing both beginners and experienced musicians to take advantage of AI in their creative process.

Here are some popular AI music tools:

1. Amper Music

Amper Music is a popular AI tool designed for creating royalty-free music. It allows users to generate custom music tracks in a variety of genres, such as electronic, cinematic, and orchestral. All you need to do is choose a mood, style, and instruments, and Amper will generate a composition tailored to your specifications. It's an excellent tool for content creators, filmmakers, and marketers looking for quick, customizable background music.

2. AIVA (Artificial Intelligence Virtual Artist)

AIVA is an AI composer that specializes in classical and cinematic music. It has been used to compose symphonies and soundtracks for films and games.

AIVA uses deep learning models to create complex and nuanced compositions, and it allows users to edit and refine the generated music. It's ideal for musicians and composers who want to explore classical or orchestral music using AI.

3. Jukedeck

Jukedeck is an AI-powered music generator that helps you create royalty-free tracks in minutes. You can choose the genre, mood, and tempo, and Jukedeck will generate a unique track for you. Jukedeck is often used by content creators, video makers, and marketers to quickly produce background music for their projects.

4. OpenAI's MuseNet

MuseNet is an advanced AI system developed by OpenAI that can generate music across a wide range of genres and instruments. Unlike simpler AI music tools, MuseNet can compose entire songs with multiple instruments, including classical music, jazz, pop, and more. MuseNet is trained on a massive dataset of diverse music, making it capable of creating complex, multi-layered compositions.

5. Soundraw

Soundraw is an AI tool that allows you to generate royalty-free music with customizable parameters. It focuses on helping content creators make personalized background music that fits their videos, games, or podcasts. You can select a genre, mood, and duration, and Soundraw will create a unique piece of music that you can download and use.

6. Magenta by Google

Magenta is an open-source project by Google that explores how AI can assist with creative processes in art and music. It offers various tools for music creation, including tools for generating melodies, harmonies, and full arrangements. Magenta also allows users to experiment with neural networks to compose music that can range from simple melodies to complex compositions.

Hands-On Activity: Create a Track Using AI Tools

Now that you understand the basics of AI in music creation and have an overview of the tools available, it's time to dive into a hands-on project. We'll guide you through the process of creating a simple AI-generated track and adding your personal touch to it.

Step 1: Choose Your AI Music Tool

For this project, we recommend starting with a tool like **Amper Music** or **Soundraw**, as they are beginner-friendly and offer customization options that are perfect for experimenting with different music styles.

1. **Sign up for Amper Music or Soundraw**: Create a free account or sign up for a trial if necessary.

2. **Choose a Genre and Mood**: Select the genre (e.g., electronic, pop, cinematic) and mood (e.g., upbeat, dramatic, relaxed) of the track you want to generate.

3. **Customize Your Track**: Adjust the tempo, key, and instrumentation to match your needs.

4. **Generate the Track**: Let the AI create a background music track based on your selected preferences.

Step 2: Review and Refine the AI-Generated Track

Once your AI-generated track is ready, take a moment to review the composition. Listen to the different sections (e.g., intro, verse, chorus, outro) and see if the track matches your expectations. AI music generators may not always hit the mark on the first try, but they provide an excellent starting point for further refinement.

1. **Identify Areas for Improvement**: Does the melody feel too repetitive? Are there any sections that need more energy or variation? Take note of areas you want to improve.

2. **Enhance the Track**: Many AI tools allow you to adjust the generated music. You can tweak the tempo, rearrange sections, or change the instrumentation to make the track more dynamic and aligned with your vision.

3. **Export the Track**: Once you're satisfied with the music, export it in a file format that suits your needs (e.g., MP3, WAV).

Step 3: Add Your Personal Touch

Now that you have your AI-generated track, it's time to add your personal touch to make it truly unique. Use a simple music production tool like **GarageBand**, **Audacity**, or **FL Studio** to enhance the track.

1. **Import the AI-Generated Music**: Upload the track into your music production software.

2. **Layer Additional Elements**: Add other instruments or effects, such as guitar riffs, vocal samples, or sound effects. This will personalize the track and make it feel more like your own creation.

3. **Mix and Master**: Adjust the levels, apply equalization, and use compression to give your track a polished sound.

Real-World Applications of AI Music Creation

AI-generated music isn't just a fun experiment—it has real-world applications across various industries, including entertainment, marketing, and content creation. Here's how AI music tools are being used today:

1. Content Creation (YouTubers, Podcasters, and Streamers)

Content creators are increasingly turning to AI music tools to create custom background music for their videos, podcasts, and streams. AI tools allow creators to generate music quickly, ensuring that their content stands out without the need for expensive licensing or the hassle of creating original compositions from scratch.

For example, a YouTuber can generate a custom track in minutes that fits the mood of their video, whether it's upbeat for a tutorial or relaxing for a travel vlog.

2. Video Game and Film Soundtracks

AI tools like AIVA and OpenAI's MuseNet are being used to compose original soundtracks for video games, films, and advertisements. These tools can generate cinematic music or theme songs tailored to a specific scene or mood. A filmmaker can quickly generate a dramatic soundtrack for a movie trailer, while game developers can use AI to create background music that adapts to the in-game environment.

3. Music for Commercials and Advertising

Marketers and advertisers use AI music to create jingles and background music for their commercials. AI allows them to generate multiple versions of a track to fit different moods or target audiences. For instance, a fast-paced jingle for a product ad can be quickly created using an AI tool like Jukedeck or

Soundraw, saving time and money while still producing high-quality content.

4. Personal Music Composition and Creative Exploration

For aspiring musicians and producers, AI provides an invaluable tool for experimentation. It allows creators to quickly explore different styles and arrangements without needing advanced musical knowledge. Whether it's producing beats, composing melodies, or generating harmonies, AI can act as a creative partner in the music composition process, providing a foundation upon which musicians can build.

Conclusion

AI is revolutionizing the music creation process, making it easier and faster to compose, produce, and refine music. With the help of AI music tools, anyone—regardless of their musical background—can create original tracks, soundtracks, jingles, and more. Whether you're a content creator looking to add custom music to your videos or an aspiring musician exploring new creative possibilities, AI is a valuable tool that can help you unlock your full musical potential.

By following the steps outlined in this chapter, you now have a practical understanding of how AI music tools work and how to apply them to your own music creation process. In the next chapter, we will dive deeper into how AI can be used for other creative processes, including graphic design and visual content creation, further enhancing your ability to create compelling multimedia content.

Chapter 6: Combining AI Tools for Your Creative Projects

Summary

As artificial intelligence continues to advance, it opens up exciting new opportunities for creators in various fields, from writing and design to music. However, the real power of AI isn't just in using a single tool but in combining multiple AI-driven tools to produce comprehensive, cohesive, and highly polished creative projects. In this chapter, we'll explore how you can integrate different AI tools for writing, design, and music to create a seamless workflow. By combining AI-powered text generation, image creation, and music composition, you can unlock new creative possibilities and drastically improve your efficiency.

You'll learn how to use these tools together to create projects that blend text, images, and sound into a unified final product. Whether you're working on a blog post with accompanying visuals, a video with an original soundtrack, or a marketing campaign that requires both graphics and text, this chapter will show you how to combine the strengths of AI tools to enhance your creative process and produce high-quality results.

Learning Objectives

By the end of this chapter, you will:

1. **Understand How to Use Multiple AI Tools Together**:
   Learn how to combine AI tools for writing, design, and music in a cohesive, efficient workflow. You will discover how AI-generated content in one area (text, images, or music) can complement the others, creating a fully integrated creative process.

2. **Learn How to Mix AI-Generated Text, Images, and Music Into a Cohesive Project**: Understand the practical steps for integrating AI-generated text, images, and music into a single project. This includes coordinating the tone, style, and aesthetic across different mediums to create a cohesive end product.

3. **Streamline Your Workflow by Combining Tools for Faster and More Creative Results**: Discover how using multiple AI tools in tandem can speed up your creative process, reduce repetitive tasks, and allow you to focus on more strategic, creative decisions. You'll see how to use AI to iterate quickly and produce polished, high-quality content in less time.

Introduction to Combining AI Tools

The true potential of AI lies in how we leverage multiple tools across different creative domains. In many creative projects, text, design, and music often go hand in hand. Whether you're developing an article, creating social media posts, producing a video, or building a presentation, the integration of AI-driven writing, design, and music can elevate your project to a whole new level.

While each AI tool can stand on its own, combining them in a coordinated way offers immense possibilities. For example, imagine you're creating a blog post or video. AI can generate the text, produce accompanying graphics, and even create a soundtrack—all seamlessly integrated to fit your theme and purpose.

The goal of this chapter is to show you how to mix and match these tools to create a streamlined, efficient creative process. We'll explore specific AI tools for writing, design, and music, and discuss how you can use them together to complete your projects faster and more effectively.

The Power of Multi-Tool Integration

Integrating multiple AI tools into one workflow can yield highly creative and professional results. For instance:

- **In Writing**: AI can generate a draft for a blog post, article, or ad copy. Once the draft is written, AI can be used to refine the text, improve readability, and adjust tone.

- **In Design**: You can use AI tools like Canva or Adobe Spark to create visually stunning images, infographics, or presentations that complement the text content you've written.

- **In Music**: AI music tools like Amper Music or Soundraw can create original background music to match the mood of your written content or visuals.

When these elements come together, you create a cohesive final product that resonates across multiple media formats.

Combining AI Writing, Design, and Music for Cohesive Projects

Let's explore how combining AI writing, design, and music tools can elevate your creative work.

Step 1: AI-Assisted Writing

AI writing tools like GPT-3 (ChatGPT), Jasper, and Copy.ai can help you generate high-quality written content in minutes. Here's how you can use these tools as the first step in your project:

1. **Generate Text with AI**: Start by choosing your topic and providing the AI with prompts. For example, if you're writing a blog post about "How AI is Changing Content Creation," you can input the prompt, "Write an introduction to a blog post about how AI is revolutionizing content creation in digital marketing."

2. **Refining the Text**: Once the AI generates the draft, use it as a foundation. Refine the content with your personal voice and style. AI tools often require human editing to ensure the tone, flow, and specific insights are aligned with your brand.

3. **Polish for SEO**: If your project is meant for online publication, use AI tools like SEMrush or Yoast SEO to optimize the content. These tools help you identify important keywords, readability scores, and meta descriptions to ensure your content performs well in search engines.

Step 2: AI-Generated Design

Once you have your text, the next step is visual design. AI design tools like Canva, Adobe Sensei, and Crello can assist in creating high-quality visuals that complement your written content. Here's how to proceed:

1. **Create Visuals with AI**: Depending on your project, you may need infographics, images, or even full presentations. Use an AI tool like Canva to create templates or backgrounds that suit your content's theme. For instance, if your blog post is about digital marketing, you might want to use a tech-inspired visual with clean lines and modern typography.

2. **Customize and Enhance**: Most AI design tools allow you to customize designs, change colors, fonts, and layouts. Experiment with different design options until you find one that complements your written content.

3. **Use AI for Image Generation**: If you want a unique image for your content, AI tools like DALL·E 2 can generate images based on your descriptions. This is especially helpful if you need an image that doesn't exist yet, like a custom graphic that illustrates a complex concept in your article.

Step 3: AI-Generated Music

Finally, music is an essential part of many projects, especially when working on videos, podcasts, or promotional content. AI music tools like Amper Music, Soundraw, and AIVA can create music that matches the tone and mood of your project. Here's how to use them:

1. **Generate Background Music**: Using an AI music generator, select a genre, mood, and tempo that fit your project. For example, if you're creating a video about AI in marketing, you might want background music that's upbeat and modern.

2. **Fine-Tune Your Track**: AI music tools often allow you to customize the track by adjusting elements like instrumentation, tempo, and length. If you want the track to transition smoothly from one section of your video to another, you can modify the music to ensure it fits perfectly.

3. **Sync Music with Visuals and Text**: If you're creating a video or presentation, synchronize the music with your visuals and written content. The right music can elevate your message,

create emotional impact, and keep your audience engaged.

Hands-On Activity: Project Creation

Now that we've explored how to use AI tools in writing, design, and music creation, let's apply what you've learned by creating a complete project.

Step 1: Choose Your Project Type

Start by deciding what type of project you want to create. You could choose a blog post with images and background music for a YouTube video, a social media post with an accompanying jingle, or even a full presentation with slides, text, and music.

For this example, let's assume you're creating a blog post about "The Future of AI in Content Creation," which will include AI-generated text, images, and background music.

Step 2: Use an AI Writing Tool for Content

1. **Generate Content**: Use a tool like ChatGPT to generate a blog post introduction and key points. You might input a prompt like, "Write a

300-word introduction to a blog post about the role of AI in the future of content creation."

2. **Refine and Edit**: After the AI generates the text, refine it by adding your voice, perspective, and personal experiences. Ensure the style and tone match your audience and purpose.

Step 3: Design Visuals Using AI

1. **Create Images**: Use a tool like Canva to create an image that aligns with your article's theme. You could design a simple infographic illustrating how AI is transforming content creation, or use AI-generated art from a tool like DALL·E to create a visual representation of the future of AI in creative industries.

2. **Integrate Your Images**: Place the AI-generated images and infographics strategically within your blog post to support the content and break up text-heavy sections.

Step 4: Generate Background Music with AI

1. **Generate Music**: Use Amper Music or Soundraw to create a background track that fits the tone of your content. For a blog post about

AI in content creation, you might want an upbeat, futuristic, or technological track.

2. **Enhance the Music**: Customize the track by adjusting the tempo or adding additional layers. You might want to add a quiet intro for the first few seconds, followed by more upbeat music once the article picks up speed.

Step 5: Compile the Complete Project

Now that you have the text, visuals, and music, it's time to integrate them into your project. Here are the final steps:

1. **Put Together Your Blog Post**: Insert the text, images, and links into your blog post template. Ensure the visuals are placed where they complement the text, and the music is set to play on background or intro sections.

2. **Publish and Share**: Once your project is complete, publish it on your website, social media, or content platform. If it's a video, share it on YouTube, Vimeo, or any other platform you're using to engage your audience.

Real-World Applications

1. Streamlining Your Workflow

One of the primary benefits of combining multiple AI tools is the ability to streamline your workflow. Instead of spending hours writing, designing, and producing music separately, AI allows you to accelerate these processes and produce high-quality content in much less time. This efficiency is crucial for content creators, marketers, and professionals who need to generate and publish content on a tight schedule.

- **Example**: A content marketer can use AI tools to generate text for a blog post, create custom images and infographics for the post, and then add background music for a video version of the blog post. This integrated workflow saves time and ensures all elements are cohesive.

2. Creative Experimentation

AI tools offer immense creative flexibility, allowing you to experiment with various styles, tones, and genres. Whether you're writing, designing, or composing music, AI gives you the freedom to explore new creative directions that might not have been possible before.

- **Example**: A YouTube creator could experiment with different AI-generated tracks, visual styles, and written content to determine what resonates best with their audience. They can iterate quickly and efficiently, trying out different combinations until they find the perfect match.

Conclusion

Combining AI tools for writing, design, and music can take your creative projects to the next level. Whether you're creating a blog post, a marketing campaign, or a video, integrating AI tools across multiple domains enables you to produce high-quality, cohesive content faster and more efficiently. By following the steps outlined in this chapter, you now have the knowledge and practical skills to incorporate AI into your creative process, ultimately enhancing your productivity and unleashing your creative potential.

Chapter 7: AI in Music— Composing, Mixing, and Mastering

Summary

Music creation is traditionally viewed as a deeply human endeavor, relying on the emotional connection between the artist and their work. However, with the rise of artificial intelligence, music composition, production, and even mastering are entering a new era, one where technology collaborates alongside human creativity. AI is not just a tool for generating melodies—it's revolutionizing every stage of music production, from initial composition to final polishing.

In this chapter, we will explore how AI is reshaping the music industry, specifically focusing on AI tools that assist with composition, arrangement, and audio enhancement. We'll dive into AI-driven software that can help you create music from scratch, assist in arranging and editing complex tracks, and even automate the mastering process for polished final results. We'll also look at how AI tools can enhance creativity, offer new perspectives on composition, and accelerate the production process—empowering musicians, producers, podcasters, and content creators to create high-quality music faster and more efficiently.

This chapter will give you the knowledge you need to understand and utilize AI tools in music composition, mixing, and mastering, ensuring you strike the right balance between AI-generated ideas and your own creative vision.

Learning Objectives

By the end of this chapter, you will:

1. **Familiarize Yourself with AI-Driven Music Composition Tools:**

Learn how AI can be leveraged to create music, whether for professional projects or personal experimentation. Explore popular AI-driven music composition tools such as Amper Music and AIVA, and understand how they can assist in the creative process.

2. **Understand How AI Assists in Audio Editing and Mastering**:
   Discover how AI-powered tools can enhance and refine your tracks, offering intelligent suggestions for mixing, mastering, and improving sound quality, making the entire music production process more efficient.

3. **Appreciate the Balance Between AI Suggestions and Creative Control**:
   Recognize the importance of maintaining creative control while using AI tools. Learn how to use AI as a creative partner rather than a replacement, ensuring your music retains its personal and artistic touch.

Introduction to AI in Music Creation and Production

The rise of AI in music creation is nothing short of transformative. In the past, producing a high-quality track involved complex knowledge of music theory, sound engineering, and long hours of manual effort. Today, AI has entered the scene as a powerful assistant, capable of assisting with everything from generating melody lines to refining audio mixes.

AI tools that generate music are powered by machine learning algorithms trained on vast amounts of music data. These algorithms learn patterns in melody, rhythm, harmony, and structure. With this data, AI can generate completely new music, whether that's a simple background track or a full orchestral composition. Beyond composition, AI is also making waves in the editing, mixing, and mastering processes, allowing musicians to refine their sound quickly and with precision.

AI in music is also helping artists and producers in ways that weren't previously possible, such as by creating custom sounds or intelligently suggesting new directions for a track. These tools provide a blend of machine efficiency and human creativity, opening up new possibilities for everyone from experienced musicians to content creators and podcasters.

AI-Driven Music Composition Tools

Let's begin by exploring some of the most popular AI tools for music composition. These tools allow musicians and producers to create music quickly, experiment with different genres, and spark new creative ideas.

1. Amper Music

Amper Music is an AI-driven platform that allows users to generate original music for any kind of project. With Amper, you can choose the mood, genre, and instrumentation of your track, and the AI will create a customized piece of music. This tool is particularly popular among content creators, filmmakers, and marketers who need original background music but don't have the time or resources to hire a composer.

- **How It Works**: Users select the genre (e.g., cinematic, electronic, pop), the mood (e.g., happy, dramatic, uplifting), and the tempo. Amper then generates the track based on these parameters. You can tweak the arrangement, instrumentation, and structure as needed.

- **Use Cases**: Content creators can use Amper to generate background music for YouTube videos, podcasts, and even commercials. The tool is easy to use and doesn't require any musical knowledge, making it accessible for non-musicians as well.

- **Limitations**: While Amper is great for generating background music, it may not always produce highly complex or nuanced compositions. For more intricate projects, musicians might need to refine the generated tracks manually.

2. AIVA (Artificial Intelligence Virtual Artist)

AIVA is an advanced AI composer that specializes in classical and cinematic music. It uses deep learning algorithms trained on a vast array of classical compositions to create original pieces of music. AIVA is especially suited for filmmakers, video game developers, and musicians who need high-quality orchestral compositions without hiring a full orchestra.

- **How It Works**: AIVA uses neural networks to analyze classical compositions, learning the intricacies of harmony, melody, and structure. The AI then applies these learned patterns to generate new music. Users can adjust the mood, genre, and style to fit their specific needs.

- **Use Cases**: AIVA is perfect for generating symphonic music for film scores, video games, and cinematic trailers. It's also used by independent composers looking for inspiration or assistance in composing large-scale orchestral pieces.

- **Limitations**: AIVA is highly focused on classical and orchestral music, so it might not be the best tool for electronic, rock, or other modern genres. However, it excels in its niche and is capable of generating complex compositions with a human-like feel.

3. Jukedeck (Now Part of TikTok's Creator Tools)

Jukedeck is a simple AI music creation tool that allows you to create original, royalty-free music by selecting a genre, mood, and tempo. It's particularly useful for video creators, marketers, and anyone in need of quick background music. TikTok's acquisition of Jukedeck signals its power and potential in the future of AI music.

- **How It Works**: Like Amper Music, Jukedeck allows you to select parameters such as genre, mood, and tempo, then generates a custom track. The tool also offers users the ability to customize the length and structure of the track.

- **Use Cases**: Jukedeck is useful for creating background music for social media videos, advertisements, and other short-form content. The simplicity of the interface makes it accessible to users with little to no music production experience.

- **Limitations**: Jukedeck is best suited for simple music generation. If you're looking for highly customizable, complex compositions, you may need to explore other tools like AIVA or Amper.

AI in Music Editing and Mastering

Once you've created your track, the next stage is refining and perfecting the sound. Here, AI can significantly improve the audio editing, mixing, and mastering process, helping musicians and producers achieve a professional sound without the need for advanced technical expertise.

1. AI Mixing Assistants (iZotope Ozone, LANDR)

AI-driven mixing tools like **iZotope Ozone** and **LANDR** can automatically analyze your track and apply the necessary adjustments to levels, EQ, compression, and other effects. These tools are designed to streamline the mixing process, making it easier to produce tracks that sound polished and professional.

- **iZotope Ozone**: Ozone is a complete suite for mixing and mastering. Its AI-powered "Master Assistant" listens to your track and makes intelligent suggestions about EQ, compression, and other effects to bring the track to life. It also offers tools to balance stereo width, add warmth, and ensure that the track sounds great on all platforms.

- **LANDR**: LANDR is another AI-powered mastering service that automatically analyzes your music and applies mastering effects to give it a polished, final sound. This tool is used by musicians and producers who need to quickly master their tracks and get them ready for distribution.

- **Use Cases**: These tools are used in the final stages of music production when mixing and mastering a track for release. They're especially useful for independent artists who may not have access to a professional sound engineer.

- **Limitations**: While AI mastering and mixing tools can produce great results in most cases, they're not a complete replacement for human expertise. A skilled audio engineer can often identify nuances and adjustments that AI tools might miss, especially for more complex or unconventional tracks.

2. AI Audio Editing Tools (Adobe Audition, Descript)

AI-powered audio editing tools like **Adobe Audition** and **Descript** help automate common editing tasks, such as removing background noise, fixing timing issues, and enhancing vocal clarity.

- **Adobe Audition**: Adobe's audio editing software features powerful AI tools for noise reduction, volume leveling, and automatic sound enhancement. It also offers real-time suggestions for improving audio quality.

- **Descript**: Descript is an innovative audio editing tool that uses AI to transcribe audio and video files, allowing you to edit audio by simply editing the text. It's perfect for podcasters and video creators who want to streamline their workflow.

- **Use Cases**: These tools are useful for cleaning up tracks, editing podcasts, or enhancing dialogue in videos. For musicians, these tools can be used to polish vocal tracks, remove unwanted noise, or improve sound clarity.

- **Limitations**: AI audio editing tools are excellent for general edits, but for more intricate and complex audio work, human intervention may still be necessary. Editing tools like these work best for polishing finished tracks rather than creating from scratch.

Balancing AI Suggestions with Creative Control

AI tools for music creation, mixing, and mastering are powerful, but they should be used in conjunction with your own creative vision. The key to using AI effectively is balancing AI's suggestions with your personal input. Here are a few tips on how to maintain control over your music while benefiting from AI assistance:

1. **Use AI for Inspiration**: Let AI help spark your creativity by generating melodies, harmonies, or beats. Once you have a solid foundation, infuse your track with personal touches, adjusting the tempo, key, and arrangement to suit your style.

2. **Experiment, Don't Rely on AI**: While AI tools can be great for producing music quickly, don't rely entirely on them. Use AI as a partner to experiment with different sounds and genres, but ensure the final piece reflects your artistic voice.

3. **Refine AI-Generated Tracks**: AI may not always get it right on the first try. Don't hesitate to refine AI-generated compositions, mixing, or

mastering suggestions. Adjust levels, add new instruments, or tweak the arrangement to make the track your own.

Hands-On Activity: AI Music Composition, Mixing, and Mastering

1. Generate a Melody with AI

Start by using a tool like **Amper Music** or **AIVA** to generate a simple melody. Choose a genre that appeals to you—whether it's electronic, classical, or cinematic—and let the AI generate a basic track.

- **Action Step**: Create a melody and experiment with the structure, adjusting sections to see how the track evolves.

2. Enhance the Music with AI Mixing Tools

Once you have a melody, import it into an AI mixing tool like **iZotope Ozone** or **LANDR**. These tools will help you refine your track by adjusting the EQ, compression, and other aspects to enhance the overall sound.

- **Action Step**: Listen to the adjustments and make manual tweaks to fine-tune the track. Pay attention to how the AI helps balance the mix and identify any areas that may need more attention.

3. Master the Track with AI Tools

Finally, use an AI mastering tool like **LANDR** to give your track the final polish. AI mastering tools ensure your track is ready for release by adjusting levels, optimizing the sound for different platforms, and improving clarity.

- **Action Step**: Run the track through a mastering tool, listen to the result, and make any final tweaks to ensure it sounds professional.

Practical Applications

AI in music is not just a novelty—it's a practical tool that's transforming the way music is created and produced. Here are some real-world applications of AI in music:

1. **Musicians Looking to Spark Creativity or Streamline Production:**
   AI tools provide an endless stream of inspiration, offering musicians new ways to

experiment with different sounds, genres, and compositions. These tools help musicians quickly generate ideas, compose melodies, and experiment with arrangements, making the production process faster and more flexible.

2. **Podcasters and Content Creators Needing Background Music**:
   AI-generated background music is an invaluable tool for podcasters, YouTubers, and content creators. Whether you need music for intros, outros, or background scoring, AI tools can generate high-quality music in minutes, saving time and money while maintaining originality.

3. **Independent Artists Exploring New Ways to Produce and Release Music Quickly**:
   For independent artists without access to large production teams, AI music tools provide a cost-effective and efficient way to produce professional tracks. These tools allow artists to generate full compositions, fine-tune their sound, and release tracks quickly, all while maintaining creative control.

Conclusion

AI is reshaping the landscape of music creation, making it easier than ever to compose, edit, and produce high-quality music. With the help of AI tools, musicians, content creators, and podcasters can generate melodies, arrange tracks, and master their compositions in record time. However, it's essential to maintain a balance between AI's suggestions and your personal creative control to ensure that your music retains its authenticity and artistic integrity.

Chapter 8: Hands-On Project— Composing and Producing a Track with AI Tools

Summary

This chapter will walk you through a practical, hands-on project to compose and produce a piece of music with the help of artificial intelligence. You'll learn how to leverage AI tools to quickly sketch out the foundational elements of a track—like melodies, harmonies, and drum patterns—and then enhance it manually in a Digital Audio Workstation (DAW). The process outlined here will help you create music that feels both professional and uniquely yours, blending AI efficiency with human creativity.

AI tools can offer musicians, producers, and content creators a great starting point, but true artistry comes from knowing how to take those initial ideas and transform them into something personal and polished. Through this project, we'll show you how to use AI to speed up the music creation process while giving you the space to add your own unique touch.

By the end of this chapter, you will have a complete, polished track that integrates AI-generated components with your creative enhancements. This track could be used as background music for a podcast, video, or even as a standalone piece for distribution.

Learning Objectives

In this hands-on project, you will:

1. **Harness an AI Composition Tool to Sketch Out a Basic Track**:
   Learn how to use an AI-driven music composition tool (such as Amper Music, AIVA, or Soundraw) to generate the foundational elements of a track, including melodies, harmonies, and rhythm.

2. **Import AI-Generated Music into a Digital Audio Workstation (DAW):**
   Gain experience in importing AI-generated music into a DAW like GarageBand, Ableton Live, or other free/low-cost software to begin refining and building the track.

3. **Apply Human Creativity in Arranging, Mixing, and Polishing the Final Piece:**
   Use your creativity to add personal touches to the AI-generated elements, such as additional instruments, lyrics, and mixing techniques to finalize the track.

Introduction to Composing and Producing Music with AI Tools

Music composition traditionally required a great deal of time, skill, and technical knowledge. With AI-driven tools, much of the complexity of generating music can now be handled by algorithms, leaving musicians with the ability to focus on the creative aspects of composition, arrangement, and production.

AI composition tools have advanced to the point where they can create fully functional tracks in minutes, with little to no musical knowledge required on the part of the user. These tools can help overcome creative blocks by suggesting chord progressions, melodies, and rhythms that fit within a given genre or mood. However, the magic happens when human creativity is applied to these AI-generated elements, refining and adjusting them to fit a specific artistic vision.

In this chapter, we'll focus on using AI for composition, followed by a manual process of enhancing the track with a DAW. While AI offers valuable assistance in creating the basic structure of a piece, your personal artistic touch will bring the track to life.

Setup: Choose a Genre or Mood for Your Composition

Before diving into AI-assisted music creation, it's important to decide on the genre or mood of the track you're aiming to produce. This decision will guide the AI tool in generating music that fits the style you're looking for. In this phase, consider the following:

1. **Choose Your Genre**:
   Are you looking to create a cinematic score, an upbeat pop track, a downtempo electronic piece, or an ambient soundscape? The genre you choose will influence the type of melody, harmony, and rhythm generated by the AI tool.

2. **Define the Mood**:
   Do you want the track to be energetic, melancholic, relaxing, or dramatic? The mood of the track should align with its intended use (e.g., background music for a podcast, soundtrack for a video, or ambient music for a game). AI tools like Amper Music allow you to select mood and tempo, ensuring the music aligns with your project's tone.

3. **Consider the Track's Purpose**:
   Are you creating background music for a specific project, such as a video or podcast? Or are you composing a standalone piece for listening or distribution? The context of your track will influence its arrangement, complexity, and length.

Example Setup:

For this project, let's assume you are creating a background track for a video that's about futuristic technology. You've chosen an electronic genre with a "futuristic" mood, and the tempo is moderate—fast enough to keep the energy up but slow enough to allow for reflection.

Once you've chosen these parameters, you're ready to start generating your music using an AI composition tool.

AI Composition: Generate the Initial Melody, Harmony, or Drum Pattern

In this section, you'll use an AI tool to generate the core elements of your track. AI-driven music tools, like **Amper Music**, **AIVA**, or **Soundraw**, allow you to generate music based on specific parameters. For example, Amper Music allows you to select genres, moods, and instruments, while AIVA specializes in creating orchestral compositions.

Step 1: Generate the Melody

1. **Using Amper Music**:
   Open Amper Music and select the genre and mood you defined earlier. Input the tempo and

duration of the track. Once you've set these parameters, let Amper generate a melody based on your inputs. You can choose the instrumentation (e.g., synthesizers, bass, drums) and adjust the complexity if needed.

2. **Using AIVA:**
   For orchestral compositions, AIVA is an excellent choice. Choose the genre (e.g., cinematic, classical) and the instruments you want to include. AIVA will generate a melody along with accompanying harmonies and structure. You can choose to refine it further if necessary.

3. **Using Soundraw:**
   Soundraw's AI allows you to adjust the mood and style of the music. Select the style that best suits your project, and Soundraw will generate a basic melody. You can then tweak the melody, tempo, and instrumentation.

Step 2: Generate Harmony and Rhythm

After generating the melody, the next step is to create harmony and rhythm. Many AI music tools allow you to add harmonic progressions and rhythmic patterns that complement the melody. Use the AI tool to generate a chord progression that fits the style and mood of your track.

- **For Example**: If you've created a melody with Amper Music in a pop style, you can add a chord progression that follows the conventions of pop music, such as I-V-vi-IV. For a cinematic track created with AIVA, the chord progression may be more complex and layered, involving modulations and harmonic shifts.

Step 3: Drum Pattern Generation

Next, you can use the AI tool to generate a basic drum pattern. Depending on the style and mood of the track, you might want a simple 4/4 kick-snare pattern or something more complex. Many AI tools provide a variety of pre-built drum patterns to choose from.

- **For Example**: In Amper Music, you can choose from various drum kits (e.g., electronic drums, acoustic drums) and let the AI generate a drum pattern that complements the melody. In AIVA, the percussion can be set to match the orchestral elements of the track.

Manual Enhancement: Add Personal Touches and Finalize the Mix

While AI-generated music can provide a strong foundation, human creativity is essential to make the track feel truly unique. This section will guide you through the process of refining and enhancing the AI-generated music in a Digital Audio Workstation (DAW).

Step 1: Import AI-Generated Music into a DAW

Once you have your AI-generated melody, harmony, and drum pattern, it's time to bring these elements into a DAW for further refinement. Some of the most popular DAWs include **GarageBand**, **Ableton Live**, **Logic Pro X**, and **FL Studio**. These platforms allow you to manipulate the tracks, add new instruments, and adjust the arrangement.

- **Action Step**: Import the AI-generated stems (individual tracks for melody, harmony, drums, etc.) into your DAW. If you generated the track in Amper Music or AIVA, download the stems and load them into your DAW for further editing.

Step 2: Enhance the Arrangement

Now, begin tweaking the track's arrangement. AI tools typically generate a simple structure (e.g., intro, verse, chorus, outro), but you can add complexity and variation to make the track more engaging.

- **Add New Instrumentation**: Introduce new instruments or sounds to the track. For example, you might add a bassline, strings, or synth pads to fill out the harmonic structure. Use your DAW to manipulate these instruments and create a fuller sound.

- **Variation in Sections**: AI tools tend to produce repetitive structures, so add variation within different sections of the track. For example, change the rhythm, add a breakdown, or experiment with dynamic changes between the verse and chorus.

Step 3: Add Lyrics (If Applicable)

If your track is more than just an instrumental background piece and you'd like to add vocals, you can now write and record lyrics. Use the AI-generated melody as the foundation for your vocal lines. If you're not a vocalist, you could collaborate with a singer or use vocal synthesis tools.

- **Action Step**: Write lyrics that complement the melody and mood of the track. Record the vocals and add them to the DAW, making adjustments to the timing and pitch if needed.

Step 4: Mixing the Track

Once you've refined the arrangement and added any additional elements (like vocals), it's time to mix the track. Mixing involves balancing the levels of each instrument, adjusting the EQ (equalization), and adding effects like reverb, delay, and compression.

- **Action Step**: Adjust the levels of each track to ensure they sit well together in the mix. Use EQ to carve out space for each instrument, making sure the bass doesn't clash with the kick drum, and the high frequencies aren't too harsh.

Step 5: Mastering the Track

The final step is mastering, where the track is optimized for playback across different devices and platforms. AI tools like **LANDR** and **iZotope Ozone** can automatically master the track, applying adjustments to the overall sound to ensure it's polished and professional.

- **Action Step**: Use an AI mastering tool to prepare the track for release. If you're using LANDR, upload the track and let the AI apply mastering effects based on the genre and mood. You can fine-tune these settings to get the perfect final sound.

Practical Applications

Let's take a look at how this process can be applied in different real-world scenarios:

1. Creating Unique Background Music for Videos or Podcasts

One of the most common uses of AI music generation is for creating background music for videos, podcasts, or livestreams. AI-generated music is quick, customizable, and often royalty-free, making it an ideal solution for creators looking to add a professional touch to their content without the need for a composer.

- **Example**: A YouTube content creator might use Amper Music to generate a background track for their tutorial video. After importing the AI-generated track into a DAW, they can adjust the track's tempo and instrumentation to fit the pacing of the video.

2. Experimenting with New Musical Styles or Collaborating with AI "Band Members"

For musicians, AI tools offer a great way to experiment with different styles or genres. If you're a pop producer who wants to try creating a cinematic score, AI tools can generate a soundtrack that serves as a starting point for your creative process. AI tools can act as "band members" that provide new ideas, harmonies, and melodies.

- **Example**: A producer who specializes in electronic music may use AIVA to compose an orchestral piece, blending classical elements with electronic beats to create a hybrid sound.

3. Independent Artists Producing and Releasing Music Quickly

For independent artists who need to produce music quickly and with minimal resources, AI tools offer a fast and cost-effective way to generate tracks. By combining AI composition tools with DAWs, independent musicians can create high-quality music without a large production team.

- **Example**: An independent artist uses Soundraw to create a unique melody and then refines the track in Ableton Live, adding personal touches like vocal effects, additional instruments, and creative arrangements.

Conclusion

AI is revolutionizing the way music is created, making it easier and faster for anyone to compose, produce, and release high-quality music. By combining AI tools for composition, arrangement, mixing, and mastering, you can quickly create music that is both professional and uniquely your own. This chapter has given you a practical, hands-on approach to working with AI in music production, empowering you to experiment, refine, and enhance your tracks with both AI assistance and human creativity.

Chapter 9: Real-World Examples of AI-Powered Content Creation

Summary

Artificial Intelligence is not just an emerging trend; it has become a transformative force in the content creation world. From writing articles and generating designs to composing music and crafting videos, AI tools are helping businesses, creators, and entrepreneurs streamline their processes, innovate faster, and produce high-quality content at scale.

In this chapter, we will dive deep into the real-world applications of AI-powered content creation. Through case studies and examples, you'll see how successful businesses and creators are using AI to enhance their work, unlock new creative possibilities, and stay ahead of trends. These examples will give you practical insights into how AI tools are being used in diverse industries like marketing, entertainment, design, journalism, and more. You'll also learn how you can apply these AI-driven strategies to your own work to maximize efficiency and creativity.

The goal of this chapter is to provide you with a comprehensive understanding of how AI is reshaping content creation in various fields and how you can harness its potential for your own projects.

Learning Objectives

By the end of this chapter, you will:

1. **See How Others Use AI Tools Creatively**: Understand how businesses, creators, and entrepreneurs are integrating AI into their content creation workflows, and discover how you can apply these insights to your own projects.

2. **Understand the Wide Range of Applications for AI in the Real World**:
   Learn about the broad spectrum of AI applications in industries such as writing, design, marketing, and entertainment, showcasing how AI is helping professionals enhance their work and stay competitive.

3. **Apply AI to Stay Ahead of Trends in Your Industry**:
   Learn how to leverage AI-powered tools to keep up with industry trends, adapt quickly to changes, and create content that resonates with your audience while staying relevant in a fast-paced, tech-driven world.

Introduction: The Growing Role of AI in Content Creation

AI is no longer the realm of science fiction. It's here, and it's reshaping industries in profound ways. Whether you're a content creator, marketer, or entrepreneur, AI tools are now a part of the everyday landscape. These tools are evolving, becoming more intuitive, and opening new avenues for creative professionals to explore.

Let's start by acknowledging the breadth of AI's impact on content creation. AI is revolutionizing every step of the content lifecycle: from ideation and writing to design, video production, and music composition. Creators are using AI to automate tedious tasks, generate creative suggestions, and produce content that would be difficult or time-consuming to create manually.

As a result, businesses and creators are able to focus on higher-level, value-added tasks—such as refining concepts, aligning content with their brand's vision, and enhancing audience engagement—while AI handles the repetitive or technical aspects.

How Businesses, Creators, and Entrepreneurs Are Using AI

In this section, we'll take a closer look at a range of real-world examples from diverse industries that illustrate how AI is being utilized to generate content, streamline workflows, and drive creativity.

1. AI-Powered Content Generation in Marketing and Advertising

One of the most significant applications of AI in content creation is in the marketing and advertising industry. AI tools are being used to generate blog posts, social media content, email campaigns, and even entire marketing strategies. Brands are leveraging AI to optimize their marketing efforts, increase efficiency, and produce personalized content for their audiences at scale.

Example: The AI-Powered Copywriting of Jasper (Formerly Jarvis)

Jasper, a leading AI writing tool, is used by marketers to create high-quality content in a fraction of the time it would take a human writer. The platform allows users to input keywords or brief descriptions, and then generates engaging, SEO-optimized copy for blogs, websites, emails, social media, and more. Jasper is powered by GPT-3, one of the most advanced AI models, which enables it to understand context, style, and tone.

Jasper has been adopted by countless businesses to improve their content marketing efforts. For example, a SaaS company might use Jasper to generate blog posts around specific keywords related to their software features, creating optimized content for SEO while maintaining a conversational tone.

Key Takeaways from Jasper's Use:

- **Efficiency**: Jasper reduces the time spent on writing, freeing up teams to focus on strategy and refining content.

- **Personalization**: AI tools like Jasper can generate personalized content that resonates with target audiences.

- **Scalability**: AI-powered writing tools help businesses scale their content marketing efforts quickly and efficiently.

2. AI for Design and Branding

In the design space, AI is being used to assist with logo creation, brand identity development, and graphic design. AI-powered design tools can help marketers and content creators produce professional-quality visuals without needing advanced graphic design skills.

Example: Canva's AI-Powered Design Suggestions

Canva, a popular design tool, uses AI to suggest design elements, color schemes, and layouts based on user input. The platform's design assistant helps users create visually appealing content such as social media graphics, presentations, and marketing materials. Canva's AI recommendations are based on design principles and trends, making it accessible to both beginners and professionals.

Many brands use Canva's AI features to create consistent, high-quality visuals across all their content. For example, a small business might use Canva to generate social media posts that align with its brand identity, ensuring that the visuals are consistent with the company's messaging and visual style.

Key Takeaways from Canva's Use:

- **Speed**: Canva's AI-powered tools allow users to create designs in minutes, saving time on manual design work.

- **Accessibility**: AI design assistants make professional design tools accessible to individuals without formal training in design.

- **Brand Consistency**: AI tools help ensure that all visual content is aligned with brand identity and style guides.

3. AI in Music Composition and Production

AI is also making a significant impact on the music industry, from composing original tracks to assisting with mixing and mastering. These tools are democratizing music creation, allowing independent musicians, content creators, and brands to produce high-quality music quickly and at scale.

Example: AI Composition Tools like AIVA and Amper Music

AIVA (Artificial Intelligence Virtual Artist) is a powerful AI tool that allows users to compose music in various genres, from classical to cinematic and electronic. The platform is used by filmmakers, video game developers, and independent musicians to generate original soundtracks and compositions. AIVA's neural network has been trained on a massive dataset of classical music, enabling it to generate sophisticated and emotionally expressive pieces.

Amper Music, on the other hand, is an AI-powered platform that lets users create original music by selecting a genre, mood, and tempo. It's widely used by content creators who need quick background music for videos, podcasts, or commercials. Both tools allow users to customize the composition by adjusting instrumentation, key, and arrangement.

Key Takeaways from AI in Music:

- **Accessibility**: AI tools make it easier for anyone to create professional-quality music, regardless of their musical training.

- **Customization**: Tools like AIVA and Amper Music allow for significant customization, enabling users to create music that fits their specific needs.

- **Speed**: AI-powered music tools significantly reduce the time required to compose and produce music, especially for content creators working on tight deadlines.

Hands-On Activity: Case Study Review

In this hands-on activity, we'll review a case study of a company or creator using AI tools to generate content. You'll explore how AI has been implemented, what challenges were overcome, and what results were achieved.

Case Study: AI in Marketing for Copywriting (Jasper)

Background: Jasper, an AI-powered writing assistant, has been used by businesses and agencies worldwide to streamline their copywriting processes. The tool leverages GPT-3 to generate text that is SEO-friendly, engaging, and tailored to specific audiences. One notable success story is its use by **Copyhackers**, a copywriting agency that wanted to enhance its content production while maintaining a high level of quality.

Challenges:

- Copyhackers had a high volume of content to produce and limited resources to maintain quality at scale.

- They needed a way to optimize content creation without compromising their unique brand voice.

Solution: Copyhackers integrated Jasper into their content workflow to assist with generating blog posts, marketing copy, email campaigns, and landing pages.

The tool helped them rapidly produce drafts that could then be refined by human writers.

Results:

- Copyhackers were able to increase content production by 40%, freeing up time for their team to focus on higher-value tasks like strategy and refining the content.

- AI-generated content maintained a high level of quality, with only minimal edits needed for tone and voice consistency.

Key Takeaways:

- **Efficiency**: Jasper significantly increased productivity by automating time-consuming tasks, allowing for quicker turnarounds.

- **Scalability**: Jasper allowed Copyhackers to scale their content production without sacrificing quality.

- **Human Creativity**: While Jasper handled the bulk of the writing, human writers were still needed to refine and ensure the content aligned with the brand voice.

Real-World Applications of AI Tools

AI-powered tools are not limited to just businesses and marketing agencies—they are transforming industries in a wide range of ways. Below are several key real-world applications where AI tools are being used to enhance content creation.

1. AI in Journalism and Newsrooms

AI is also making waves in journalism, where it's being used to generate news articles, summaries, and data-driven content. AI tools can quickly analyze data, identify trends, and produce news reports without the need for human journalists to spend hours collecting and processing the information.

Example: The Washington Post's Heliograf AI
The Washington Post uses Heliograf, an AI-powered tool, to generate real-time news updates and reports on topics like sports, election results, and financial markets. The tool allows journalists to focus on more complex stories while AI handles routine reporting.

2. AI for Social Media Content Creation

AI is revolutionizing the way brands create social media content. Platforms like **Lately.ai** use AI to analyze previous posts and generate content that is likely to resonate with an audience. This makes it easier for marketers to maintain an active social media presence without manually creating every post.

3. AI for Video Creation and Editing

In the world of video production, AI tools like **Magisto** and **Piktochart** are used to automatically generate videos from raw footage. These tools analyze the video content, apply effects, and sync it with music, making it easier for businesses and content creators to produce videos quickly.

4. AI for Interactive and Personalized Content

Personalization is one of the biggest trends in content marketing, and AI plays a pivotal role in this. Tools like **Persado** use AI to generate personalized email subject lines, social media ads, and marketing messages tailored to individual users based on their behavior, preferences, and past interactions.

How to Use AI Tools to Stay Ahead of Trends in Your Industry

As AI continues to evolve, it's essential for businesses, creators, and entrepreneurs to stay ahead of the curve. Here are some strategies for leveraging AI tools to remain competitive and innovative:

1. **Embrace AI as a Creative Partner:**
   Instead of seeing AI as a replacement for human creativity, view it as a tool that enhances your ability to generate new ideas and iterate on existing concepts. AI can help you push boundaries and explore creative possibilities you might not have considered before.

2. **Automate Repetitive Tasks:**
   Use AI to automate time-consuming and repetitive tasks, such as content generation, image creation, and video editing. This will allow you to focus on higher-level strategic tasks that require your expertise and creativity.

3. **Analyze Data to Improve Content:**
   AI tools can provide insights into how your content is performing and what your audience

prefers. Use this data to optimize your content strategy, improve engagement, and stay ahead of the competition.

4. **Stay Agile and Adapt Quickly**:
   AI tools can help you keep up with trends and shifts in your industry. By leveraging AI-driven insights, you can quickly adapt your content strategy to changing audience preferences, new technology, or emerging market demands.

Conclusion

AI-powered content creation is no longer a novelty— it's a vital tool used by businesses, creators, and entrepreneurs to produce high-quality content efficiently and at scale. From writing and design to music composition and video production, AI is transforming industries and unlocking new creative possibilities. By learning from real-world examples and integrating AI into your own workflow, you can stay ahead of trends, increase productivity, and produce content that resonates with your audience.

Chapter 10: Building Your Portfolio with AI Projects

Summary

In the fast-evolving world of artificial intelligence, the ability to harness AI tools to create content has become a powerful asset. As more businesses, agencies, and individual creators adopt AI technologies to streamline their workflows and enhance their creative output, the demand for professionals who can effectively use these tools is growing. Building a portfolio that showcases your AI-generated work is an essential step in positioning yourself as a forward-thinking professional in the creative fields.

This chapter will guide you through the process of creating a standout portfolio that highlights your best AI-powered writing, design, and music projects. We'll provide you with tips on how to present your AI projects to clients or employers, ensuring that you effectively communicate the value of your work and demonstrate your skills with confidence. By the end of this chapter, you'll have the knowledge and practical skills needed to create a polished, professional portfolio that reflects your expertise in AI-assisted content creation.

Learning Objectives

By the end of this chapter, you will:

1. **Learn How to Build a Strong Portfolio That Includes AI-Powered Content:**
   Understand the best practices for selecting and presenting your best AI-generated work in a way that highlights your creative skills and technical proficiency.

2. **Understand How to Talk About Your AI Projects in a Professional Way:**
   Learn how to effectively communicate the

process, value, and outcomes of your AI-driven projects to clients, employers, or potential collaborators.

3. **Create a Portfolio and Showcase Your Work**: Gain hands-on experience in putting together a small portfolio of AI-generated content, whether it's writing, design, or music, and learn how to present it online.

Introduction: The Importance of AI in Building a Modern Portfolio

As AI technologies continue to advance, the ability to leverage these tools in creative work is becoming an increasingly sought-after skill. Many industries—from marketing and design to content creation and music production—are using AI tools to enhance their workflows and produce high-quality results more efficiently. If you can demonstrate your ability to integrate AI into your creative projects, you're positioning yourself as a professional who's both innovative and adaptable.

Building a portfolio that showcases your AI-powered projects not only demonstrates your technical abilities but also shows that you're able to combine technology with creativity to produce impactful work. The AI-driven portfolio has the potential to set you apart in a crowded job market, attract clients, and open up new career opportunities. Whether you're a freelance writer, a graphic designer, a music producer, or an entrepreneur, your portfolio is your personal brand, and showcasing your AI skills is a strategic way to enhance it.

The Building Blocks of an AI-Driven Portfolio

An AI-driven portfolio is a collection of work that highlights your ability to use AI tools effectively in creative projects. Depending on your area of expertise—whether it's writing, design, music, or another field—the portfolio can showcase a variety of AI-generated content.

1. Showcase a Range of Work

A strong AI-powered portfolio should include a diverse set of projects that demonstrate the range of your skills. For instance, if you're a content creator, your portfolio might include:

- **AI-Generated Writing**: Blog posts, marketing copy, email campaigns, or social media content.

- **AI-Generated Design**: Logos, banners, social media posts, or website designs created using AI-powered design tools like Canva or Adobe Sensei.

- **AI-Generated Music**: Background tracks for videos or podcasts, original music compositions, or jingles created using AI tools like Amper Music or AIVA.

2. Choose the Best Examples

Your portfolio should highlight the projects that best showcase your proficiency with AI tools. Choose work that demonstrates not only technical expertise but also creativity and originality. Remember, quality over quantity is key.

3. Display the AI Tools Used

It's important to highlight the AI tools you used for each project. This will help potential clients or employers understand your level of familiarity with different AI platforms and technologies. For example, if you used **Jasper** for writing or **Amper Music** for music creation, mention these tools and explain how they contributed to the final project.

4. Show Your Creative Process

A great way to set your portfolio apart is by showcasing your process, especially if it involves integrating AI tools. Show how you used AI to assist in brainstorming ideas, drafting, designing, or editing, and then applied your own creative flair to refine and personalize the output. This will demonstrate that you can effectively use AI as a creative partner rather than a mere assistant.

How to Talk About Your AI Projects Professionally

As AI tools become more commonplace, it's essential to be able to speak about your AI-powered projects confidently and professionally. Potential clients, collaborators, or employers may not fully understand the scope or value of AI-generated content, so it's crucial to explain both the process and the outcomes.

1. Highlight the Value of AI in the Process

Start by explaining how AI improved the efficiency and quality of the project. For example, you can say:

- "By using **Amper Music**, I was able to quickly generate a custom track that fit the mood of the video, which saved significant time compared to composing from scratch. I then added my own elements to create a unique soundscape."

This statement shows that you're using AI to enhance your workflow rather than relying solely on automation.

2. Explain the Tools You Used

Be specific about the AI tools you used. For example:

- "For this graphic design project, I used **Canva's AI-powered design assistant** to create an eye-catching social media ad. The tool suggested color palettes and fonts, which I then fine-tuned to match the brand's visual identity."

Detailing the tools you've used helps potential clients or employers see your technical expertise and your ability to work with cutting-edge technology.

3. Demonstrate the Impact of AI on Your Work

Explain how AI positively impacted the outcome of the project. For example:

- "AI allowed me to generate several writing drafts quickly, which enabled me to focus on refining the content and aligning it with the client's brand voice. This resulted in a faster turnaround time and improved overall quality."

By framing AI as a tool that enhances creativity and productivity, you can demonstrate your value to potential clients or employers.

Hands-On Activity: Create a Portfolio

Now, let's put theory into practice. In this hands-on activity, you'll create a small portfolio of your best AI-powered work. This could be a mix of writing, design, or music, depending on your area of expertise.

Step 1: Choose Your Best AI-Generated Work

Select the best projects you've worked on that demonstrate your use of AI tools. These could be:

- **AI Writing Projects**: Blog posts, ad copy, social media posts, or marketing emails you've generated using AI tools like **Jasper** or **Copy.ai**.

- **AI Design Projects**: Graphics, posters, logos, or social media content you've designed using tools like **Canva**, **Crello**, or **Adobe Spark**.

- **AI Music Projects**: Tracks or jingles you've created with tools like **Amper Music**, **AIVA**, or **Soundraw**.

Step 2: Organize and Present Your Work

Now that you've selected your projects, it's time to organize them in a cohesive and professional manner. Here are some steps for presenting your work:

1. **Create a Simple Website or Portfolio Page**: Use website builders like **Wix**, **Squarespace**, or **WordPress** to create a portfolio website. These platforms often come with templates that make it easy to showcase your work in an attractive layout.

2. **Provide Context for Each Project**: For each project, include a brief description of the work, the AI tools used, and how AI contributed to the

final result. Explain the creative process, the challenges faced, and how you overcame them.

3. **Add Samples or Previews**: Depending on the medium, add relevant samples or previews of your work. For written content, provide excerpts. For design projects, include images or interactive demos. For music projects, embed sound clips or links to platforms like **SoundCloud** or **YouTube**.

4. **Include Testimonials (If Applicable)**: If you've worked with clients or collaborators, consider including brief testimonials that speak to your ability to work with AI tools. This adds credibility and shows that your work has made a positive impact.

Step 3: Make Your Portfolio Accessible

To showcase your work effectively, ensure that your portfolio is accessible to potential clients, employers, or collaborators. Here are some tips for promoting your portfolio:

1. **Link to Your Portfolio on Your Resume and Social Media**: Share the link to your portfolio on

your professional resume, LinkedIn profile, and any other platforms where you network.

2. **Optimize Your Portfolio for SEO**: Use relevant keywords on your website to ensure it ranks well on search engines. Include terms related to AI content creation, such as "AI writing," "AI design," or "AI music production."

3. **Use Interactive Elements**: If possible, use interactive elements (such as embedded music or scrollable designs) to keep visitors engaged. This shows not only your creativity but also your technical skills.

Real-World Applications

AI tools can help you build a portfolio that stands out in the competitive world of content creation. Here are a few real-world applications of how an AI-powered portfolio can benefit you:

1. Building a Professional Portfolio for Job Opportunities

AI-powered portfolios are ideal for job seekers who want to demonstrate their technical skills. Whether you're applying for a content creation role, a marketing position, or a design job, showcasing your ability to use AI tools in your work can set you apart from other candidates.

Example: A graphic designer might use AI-powered tools like **Canva** and **Adobe Sensei** to generate original designs for clients. By including these designs in their portfolio and explaining how AI enhanced the creative process, the designer can show their proficiency with modern tools and stand out to potential employers.

2. Attracting Clients as a Freelancer

Freelancers can use AI-powered portfolios to demonstrate their versatility and efficiency. AI tools can help you deliver high-quality content faster, which is especially valuable in industries like marketing, advertising, and content creation.

Example: A freelance writer who uses **Jasper** to generate copy quickly can showcase their efficiency in their portfolio, offering potential clients a faster turnaround without sacrificing quality. By demonstrating this, the freelancer can attract more business.

3. Gaining Recognition as an AI-Driven Creator

For creators in music, design, or writing, having an AI-powered portfolio shows that you are embracing the future of creative work. It positions you as a forward-thinking artist who understands the power of new technologies.

Example: An independent musician who uses **Amper Music** to compose original tracks and then refines them in a DAW could showcase these tracks on their portfolio, highlighting their ability to collaborate with AI tools to produce high-quality, unique music.

Conclusion

Building a portfolio with AI-generated content is an essential step in showcasing your creativity and technical prowess in today's fast-evolving job market. Whether you're a writer, designer, musician, or entrepreneur, presenting AI-powered projects demonstrates that you are not only proficient with modern tools but also adaptable and forward-thinking. By following the strategies outlined in this chapter, you can build a professional, polished portfolio that helps you stand out and attract the opportunities you deserve.

Chapter 11: AI Tools You Need to Know

Summary

Artificial Intelligence is transforming how content is created across a variety of fields, including writing, design, and music. Whether you're an entrepreneur, freelancer, or seasoned creative professional, AI tools are now indispensable in accelerating the creative process and unlocking new possibilities. However, with so many AI-powered platforms available, it can be overwhelming to choose the right ones for your specific needs. This chapter is designed to help you navigate this landscape by highlighting the best AI tools for writing, design, and music creation, and offering tips on how to select the ones that best fit your creative style and workflow.

We'll dive into the top AI tools in each category, from AI-assisted writing platforms to design assistants and music composition tools. With the right tools at your disposal, you can streamline your workflow, experiment with new ideas, and create professional-grade content faster than ever before.

Learning Objectives

By the end of this chapter, you will:

1. **Get Familiar with Top AI Tools in Different Areas of Content Creation**:
   Learn about the most effective AI tools in writing, design, and music, and how they can support your creative process.

2. **Learn How to Pick Tools That Fit Your Creative Style**:
   Understand how to assess AI tools based on your specific needs, workflow, and the types of content you create.

3. **Improve Your Creative Process by Using the Best AI Tools**:
   Gain practical insights into how to integrate the

right AI tools into your workflow to increase efficiency and enhance creativity.

Introduction: The Power of AI Tools in Creative Work

The rise of artificial intelligence has brought with it an explosion of innovative tools that can help creators produce high-quality work faster, more efficiently, and with greater creative flexibility. Whether you are a writer crafting blog posts, a designer working on marketing materials, or a musician composing tracks, AI-powered tools are revolutionizing the way content is created.

AI tools are not a replacement for human creativity, but rather a means of enhancing it. These tools can handle repetitive tasks, generate ideas, suggest improvements, and even provide entire drafts of text, designs, or melodies. By leveraging AI tools, you can focus on higher-level tasks such as refining concepts, aligning your work with your audience's needs, and pushing the boundaries of your creative capabilities.

However, with a vast range of AI tools available, it's essential to choose the right ones for your specific needs. This chapter will provide an overview of the best AI tools in writing, design, and music creation, offering guidance on how to select the tools that will make a difference in your creative process.

Top AI Tools for Writing

AI-powered writing tools are among the most popular and widely used in the creative industry. These tools can help you write faster, refine your content, and generate ideas for your projects. Let's take a closer look at the most effective AI tools for writers.

1. Jasper (formerly Jarvis)

Jasper is one of the most popular AI writing assistants available. Powered by GPT-3, it can generate high-quality content for a variety of purposes, from blog posts and social media copy to email marketing and product descriptions.

- **Features:**
    - AI-generated blog posts, articles, and ad copy
    - SEO-friendly content suggestions

- o   A wide range of templates for different content types

- o   Ability to adjust tone, style, and complexity based on user input

- o   Content rewriting and summarization capabilities

- **Why it's Great**: Jasper is designed to help you quickly generate content, making it an ideal tool for marketers, bloggers, and content creators. Its ability to understand context and generate human-like text ensures your content is engaging and readable.

- **Best For**: Bloggers, marketers, and businesses looking to produce high-quality written content quickly.

2. Copy.ai

Copy.ai is another AI-powered writing tool that focuses on marketing content. Like Jasper, Copy.ai uses GPT-3 to generate compelling copy, and it offers a variety of templates to assist with writing product descriptions, social media ads, and email campaigns.

- **Features:**

- o AI-generated headlines, social media posts, and email copy

- o Easy-to-use templates for different content types

- o Collaboration tools for team-based writing

- o Built-in brainstorming features for idea generation

- **Why it's Great**: Copy.ai is known for its simplicity and ease of use. Its ability to generate high-converting copy quickly makes it a valuable tool for marketing teams and entrepreneurs.

- **Best For**: Marketers, copywriters, and business owners who need fast, effective copy for advertisements and campaigns.

3. Grammarly

Grammarly is a popular AI-powered grammar and writing assistant. It helps users improve their writing by suggesting corrections for spelling, grammar, style, and tone. While not a content generator like Jasper or

Copy.ai, Grammarly is an essential tool for anyone looking to polish their writing.

- **Features:**
  - Grammar, spelling, and punctuation corrections
  - Tone analysis and style suggestions
  - Clarity improvements and readability enhancements
  - Plagiarism checker (Premium version)

- **Why it's Great**: Grammarly excels at making your writing cleaner and more professional. Whether you're writing a blog post, an email, or a formal document, Grammarly helps ensure your content is error-free and optimized for readability.

- **Best For**: Writers, students, and professionals looking to refine and polish their writing.

Top AI Tools for Design

In the world of design, AI is being used to enhance creativity, streamline workflows, and generate high-quality visuals quickly. Let's take a look at some of the best AI-powered design tools available.

1. Canva

Canva is one of the most user-friendly design tools available, and it integrates AI to help users create beautiful designs quickly and easily. Canva's AI-powered design assistant offers suggestions for color schemes, fonts, and layouts, making it ideal for both beginner and experienced designers.

- **Features**:
    - Easy drag-and-drop design interface
    - AI-powered templates and design suggestions
    - Image editing tools, including background removal
    - Collaboration features for team-based design projects
- **Why it's Great**: Canva simplifies design for anyone, regardless of skill level. Its AI-powered recommendations help users create visually appealing content in minutes, making it a great

tool for social media managers, marketers, and small businesses.

- **Best For**: Small business owners, social media managers, and content creators who need quick, professional-looking designs.

2. Adobe Sensei

Adobe Sensei is Adobe's AI and machine learning platform, integrated into many of Adobe's creative tools. Sensei powers features like auto-tagging images, face recognition, and content-aware fills, helping designers save time and improve their workflows.

- **Features**:
  - AI-powered image recognition and categorization
  - Automatic tagging of assets based on content
  - Intelligent content-aware fills for photo editing
  - Facial recognition for portrait design and adjustments

- **Why it's Great**: Adobe Sensei is perfect for designers who want to leverage the power of AI within the Adobe Creative Cloud suite. It enhances productivity by automating time-consuming tasks, allowing designers to focus on the creative aspects of their work.

- **Best For**: Professional designers who use Adobe products and want to leverage AI to automate tasks and streamline their workflow.

3. Crello (VistaCreate)

Crello is a design tool similar to Canva, offering AI-powered templates for social media posts, advertisements, and other types of visual content. Its extensive library of templates and design elements makes it a great choice for businesses and marketers who need to produce high-quality visuals quickly.

- **Features**:
    - Pre-designed templates for social media, ads, and presentations
    - AI-powered design suggestions and automated resizing

- o Animation tools for creating dynamic content

- o Access to a library of stock photos, videos, and music

- **Why it's Great**: Crello offers a comprehensive set of tools for content creators, with AI features that make it easier to design and customize visual content. Its user-friendly interface ensures that anyone can create professional-level designs without prior experience.

- **Best For**: Entrepreneurs, marketers, and businesses that need visually compelling content for social media, advertising, and branding.

Top AI Tools for Music Creation

In the world of music, AI is providing exciting new ways to compose, arrange, and produce tracks. Whether you're creating background music for a project or composing a full song, these AI tools can help you streamline the process and generate high-quality music.

1. Amper Music

Amper Music is an AI-powered music composition platform that enables users to create original music without needing to know how to play an instrument. With Amper, you can choose a genre, mood, and tempo, and the AI will generate a custom track for you. It's widely used by content creators who need royalty-free music for videos, podcasts, and advertisements.

- **Features**:
  - AI-generated custom music based on user input (genre, mood, tempo)
  - Easy integration with video editing tools
  - Adjustable arrangements and instrumentals
  - Licensing for royalty-free use in commercial projects

- **Why it's Great**: Amper Music is ideal for anyone looking to create high-quality music quickly. It simplifies music production by allowing users to generate full tracks in minutes, without the need for complex music production software.

- **Best For**: Content creators, filmmakers, and marketers who need background music for their videos and advertisements.

2. AIVA (Artificial Intelligence Virtual Artist)

AIVA is an AI music composition tool that specializes in creating orchestral music. It's been used to compose soundtracks for films, video games, and advertisements. AIVA allows users to select the genre, mood, and instruments they want in their composition, and then generates an original piece based on these parameters.

- **Features**:
  - AI-generated orchestral and cinematic compositions
  - Full control over tempo, key, and instrumentation
  - Ability to export MIDI files for further editing
  - AI suggestions for melodies and harmonies
- **Why it's Great**: AIVA excels at creating complex, emotional compositions, particularly

for orchestral and cinematic music. It's perfect for film composers, game developers, and anyone who needs large-scale compositions for multimedia projects.

- **Best For**: Musicians, composers, and video producers working in the cinematic, gaming, or film industries who need original orchestral music.

3. Soundraw

Soundraw is an AI music generation tool that allows users to create original, royalty-free music for a variety of projects. Unlike some other music tools, Soundraw offers a lot of customization, allowing users to control the mood, genre, and arrangement of the track.

- **Features:**
  - Customizable genre, mood, and tempo
  - Multiple arrangement styles for track composition
  - Instant previews of generated music
  - Music creation for a variety of use cases (YouTube videos, podcasts, etc.)

- **Why it's Great**: Soundraw offers a unique blend of customization and ease of use, making it a great choice for creators who need personalized music quickly. The platform's simple interface and royalty-free licensing make it ideal for content creators.

- **Best For**: Content creators, podcasters, and marketers who need personalized background music for their projects.

Hands-On Activity: Tool Exploration

Now that you're familiar with the top AI tools in writing, design, and music creation, it's time to test them out yourself. In this hands-on activity, you will experiment with at least two AI tools from different categories (writing, design, or music) to see which ones suit your creative needs.

Step 1: Choose Your AI Tools

Select two or three AI tools from different categories. For example:

- **For Writing**: Try using Jasper or Copy.ai to generate a blog post or ad copy.

- **For Design**: Experiment with Canva or Crello to create a social media graphic or poster.

- **For Music**: Use Amper Music or Soundraw to generate background music for a project.

Step 2: Test the Tools

Experiment with each tool, testing how well they generate content based on your input. Adjust parameters such as genre, mood, tempo (for music), or tone, and evaluate the results.

- **Writing**: Generate a blog post, email, or social media content using an AI writing tool. Refine it based on your personal style and preferences.

- **Design**: Create a visual using AI-powered design tools. Test different templates and make adjustments to colors, fonts, and layouts.

- **Music**: Generate a piece of music using an AI music tool. Customize the arrangement and export the track for further use.

Step 3: Evaluate the Tools

After testing the tools, evaluate how well each one met your needs. Consider the following:

- How intuitive was the tool to use?

- Did the generated content meet your expectations?

- How easy was it to refine or customize the output?

Based on your evaluation, decide which tools best suit your creative style and workflow.

Real-World Applications

The tools you choose will directly impact how you work, whether you're building your portfolio, creating content for clients, or experimenting with new ideas. Here are a few real-world applications:

1. For Freelancers and Entrepreneurs

AI tools help freelancers and small business owners work efficiently and competitively. Whether you're a writer creating copy for clients, a designer producing branding materials, or a musician creating custom tracks, AI tools enable you to complete projects quickly without compromising quality.

2. For Marketers and Content Creators

Marketers and content creators use AI tools to streamline content creation, enhance productivity, and engage with their audience more effectively. AI can assist in writing blog posts, generating social media graphics, or producing background music, helping content creators stay on top of their content schedules.

3. For Agencies and Large Enterprises

Agencies use AI tools to handle large volumes of content creation, marketing, and design projects for multiple clients. With AI, teams can generate high-quality work faster, enabling them to take on more projects and deliver results more efficiently.

Conclusion

AI tools are transforming the content creation process by enabling professionals to work faster, enhance their creativity, and generate high-quality work. By understanding the best AI tools available and selecting the ones that suit your needs, you can improve your workflow, produce content more efficiently, and stay ahead of industry trends. The tools discussed in this chapter offer a powerful foundation for building a creative and effective workflow, helping you create content that stands out in a competitive market.

Chapter 12: Staying Creative with AI

Summary

Artificial Intelligence (AI) has become a vital part of many creative industries, empowering creators to enhance their workflows, generate new ideas, and produce high-quality content at an unprecedented pace. But as we increasingly rely on AI tools, the challenge arises of maintaining our creative edge. How can we use AI as a tool without letting it overshadow our unique vision and artistic flair? This chapter addresses this critical balance, offering strategies to ensure that AI enhances rather than diminishes your creativity. It's not about allowing AI to dictate your work, but about using it to push your ideas further, refine your concepts, and elevate your process.

By learning how to integrate AI into your creative work in a way that amplifies your personal style, you can stay ahead of the curve while still maintaining control over the artistic elements that make your work truly yours. In this chapter, we will explore the concept of AI as a creative partner, discuss how to blend AI-generated content with your ideas, and offer practical tips for staying creative while working with AI tools.

Learning Objectives

By the end of this chapter, you will:

1. **Learn How to Balance AI Assistance with Your Own Ideas**:
   Understand how to use AI as a complement to your creativity, ensuring that the final output reflects your personal style and vision.

2. **Discover Ways to Make AI Part of Your Creative Process Without Losing Your Personal Touch**:
   Learn strategies for integrating AI into your creative workflow while preserving the unique elements that make your work stand out.

3. **Use AI to Spark Creativity and Push Boundaries**:
   Find ways to leverage AI tools as sources of inspiration and innovation that challenge your creative boundaries, helping you think in new ways and experiment with ideas you may not have considered.

Introduction: AI as a Creative Partner

In the world of content creation, AI has shifted from being a purely technical tool to a creative one. Whether you're a writer, designer, musician, or any other kind of creator, AI has become an indispensable part of the creative process. But the true power of AI lies in how we choose to use it. It can be an incredible asset if it's integrated thoughtfully into our creative workflow, but it can also risk stifling creativity if it's relied upon too heavily or used in a way that limits personal expression.

AI can handle mundane, repetitive tasks—like generating draft text, suggesting design elements, or producing basic music tracks—freeing up time for creators to focus on the more nuanced and emotional aspects of their work. However, AI is not a replacement for human creativity. It's essential to remember that your unique perspective, intuition, and artistic sensibility are irreplaceable and should be at the heart of your process.

This chapter is about striking that delicate balance—leveraging AI as a powerful assistant, while still ensuring that your creative spirit and individuality shine through in everything you create.

How to Balance AI Assistance with Your Own Ideas

AI tools are becoming more sophisticated, and they can undoubtedly save creators significant time and effort. However, when it comes to creativity, AI is best viewed as a facilitator, not a substitute. Here are some practical ways to use AI to complement your ideas and maintain a healthy balance between technology and your creative instincts.

1. Use AI for Idea Generation, But Add Your Own Twist

AI tools can help you brainstorm ideas, generate potential concepts, and even suggest new angles for your projects. But while AI can provide the raw material, it's up to you to shape it, refine it, and give it meaning.

For example, AI tools like **Jasper** or **Copy.ai** can quickly generate blog post ideas, ad copy, or creative writing prompts based on a few input keywords. But it's your unique perspective that can transform those ideas into something truly distinctive. You can take an AI-generated outline, for instance, and mold it into something that aligns with your voice and your audience's needs. By infusing your personality, values, and goals into the AI suggestions, you create content that feels authentic and engaging.

2. Set Boundaries for AI Involvement

AI can be an invaluable asset, but it's important to set clear boundaries regarding where you want the AI to step in and where you want to retain full control. For example, in writing, AI can be used to generate the first draft, but you might choose to refine the tone, adjust the structure, and incorporate personal insights that only you can provide. Similarly, in design, AI can suggest layout and color palette options, but you should take ownership of the final design to ensure it aligns with your aesthetic and messaging.

By setting boundaries, you maintain control over the parts of the project that matter most to you while allowing AI to handle the more mechanical tasks.

3. Embrace AI for Efficiency, Not as a Shortcut

AI is great for enhancing efficiency, especially when it comes to tasks like content creation, editing, and ideation. However, don't fall into the trap of using AI as a shortcut to avoid doing the deeper work yourself. True creativity often comes from engaging with your ideas, wrestling with them, and refining them over time. AI can speed up processes like drafting, idea generation, and pattern recognition, but it should not replace the depth of thought, experimentation, and emotional connection that fuels your creative work.

For example, AI-generated music can give you a great starting point, but adding unique instrumental layers, adjusting dynamics, and fine-tuning the arrangement requires your artistic touch. Similarly, AI-generated design can produce excellent mockups, but you are the one who brings those designs to life with your vision and experience.

Creative Exercise: Using AI to Help Brainstorm Ideas

To put theory into practice, let's start with a creative exercise. In this activity, you will use AI to help brainstorm ideas, but you will ensure that the final concept is uniquely yours.

Step 1: Brainstorm Using AI

Use an AI tool like **Jasper** (for writing), **Canva** (for design), or **Amper Music** (for music) to generate some initial ideas for a project. For example, you might ask **Jasper** to help brainstorm ideas for a blog post on "The Future of Artificial Intelligence in Design," or you could ask **Amper Music** to generate a basic melody for a futuristic soundtrack.

Step 2: Add Your Own Creative Twist

Once the AI provides suggestions, take those ideas and refine them according to your personal creative vision. In the case of writing, adjust the tone or angle to align with your brand's voice. For music, experiment with different instrumentation, tempo, or genre to give the AI-generated track your personal flair. For design, customize the template and layout to better reflect your unique style and the message you want to convey.

Step 3: Evaluate and Reflect

After completing the exercise, evaluate the final output. How did AI assist you in the brainstorming process? What personal elements did you add to the AI-generated content to make it your own? Reflect on how the combination of AI-generated suggestions and your own creativity produced a unique and effective result.

Creative Strategies for Blending AI with Your Personal Style

Once you've experienced the balance between AI input and human creativity, it's time to consider how you can consistently integrate AI into your creative process without losing your personal touch. Below are a few strategies to keep the balance intact while using AI as a tool to enhance your creative capabilities.

1. Think of AI as Your Assistant, Not Your Creator

AI should be seen as a supportive tool rather than the driver of the creative process. It can help generate ideas, provide suggestions, and refine your work, but the vision, emotional depth, and personal connection must come from you. Embrace AI as an assistant that helps bring your ideas to life, but keep the creative direction in your hands.

2. Set Clear Intentions for AI Integration

Before using AI, set clear intentions for how it should be used. Are you using AI to speed up the writing process, generate ideas, or assist with editing? Are you relying on AI to create background music or to suggest visual layouts? Setting clear intentions helps ensure that AI contributes in a meaningful way without taking over the creative process.

3. Keep Iterating and Refining

AI can give you a great starting point, but the real magic happens when you take that starting point and continue iterating. Don't accept the AI-generated content as final—tweak it, refine it, and make it yours. Whether it's adding your personal style to a blog post, modifying a design to reflect your brand's identity, or adjusting a piece of music to match the mood of your project, always make sure to put your creative stamp on the work.

Real-World Applications: Using AI to Spark Creativity and Push Boundaries

AI tools are not just about enhancing efficiency—they can also serve as a catalyst for creativity. Here are a few real-world applications where AI can help spark creativity and push the boundaries of your work.

1. Generating New Ideas and Concepts

AI tools are excellent at helping you brainstorm fresh ideas. Whether you're struggling to come up with a new blog post topic, seeking innovative design concepts, or trying to write lyrics for a song, AI can quickly generate a variety of suggestions to get you started. These suggestions might not always be perfect, but they can help you see things from a different perspective and spark new ideas.

2. Breaking Creative Blocks

Sometimes, the hardest part of the creative process is overcoming a mental block. AI can provide a quick and efficient way to break through these blocks. For example, if you're stuck while writing a story, an AI writing tool can generate a plot twist or a new character idea. In design, AI can offer visual elements that you might not have considered, giving you the inspiration needed to move forward.

3. Expanding Creative Horizons

AI can help you experiment with new styles, techniques, and genres that you may not have explored on your own. By using AI to push the boundaries of your creativity, you can break free from conventional approaches and experiment with new ideas. Whether you're using AI to blend genres in music, explore different visual styles in design, or combine writing techniques, AI can encourage you to step outside your comfort zone and explore uncharted creative territory.

Conclusion

AI is a powerful tool that can greatly enhance your creative process, but it's crucial to maintain your unique creative voice. By using AI as a partner rather than a replacement, you can take advantage of its capabilities while still retaining control over the artistic aspects of your work. This chapter has shown you how to balance AI assistance with your own ideas, ensuring that your work reflects both your creativity and the power of AI tools.

Chapter 13: The Future of AI in Content Creation

Summary

As AI technology continues to evolve at a rapid pace, its impact on content creation is only becoming more profound. From writing and design to music and video production, AI is transforming how we create, collaborate, and innovate. However, as AI tools improve, new opportunities and challenges will arise, fundamentally changing the way creators approach their work. In this chapter, we will explore what's next for AI in creative fields, uncover emerging trends, and delve into the possibilities of new AI-powered tools that could shape the future of content creation.

AI's role in creativity is no longer just a passing trend—it's the foundation for the next wave of innovation in creative industries. By understanding the emerging technologies and trends, you can stay ahead of the curve and position yourself as a leader in this evolving landscape. This chapter aims to provide you with the insights needed to future-proof your creative career, understand the opportunities on the horizon, and adapt to the changing needs of the content creation industry.

Learning Objectives

By the end of this chapter, you will:

1. **Stay Ahead by Understanding Emerging AI Technologies**:
   Learn about the latest AI advancements in content creation and how they're transforming industries.

2. **Understand the Future Possibilities of AI in Writing, Design, and Music**:
   Gain insight into upcoming trends, tools, and applications in AI across creative fields such as writing, design, and music composition.

3. **Prepare for the Future of AI and Stay Competitive in Your Creative Field**:
    Learn how to future-proof your creative skills, adapt to new AI tools, and stay competitive in a rapidly evolving content creation landscape.

Introduction: The Unstoppable Rise of AI in Creative Industries

AI has already begun revolutionizing how we approach content creation, providing new opportunities for creators across every sector. While tools like GPT-3 for writing, DALL·E for design, and Amper Music for music composition have been transformative, the future holds even more exciting possibilities. AI is set to not only streamline workflows but also unlock new levels of creativity, allowing creators to push boundaries in ways that were previously unimaginable.

To stay competitive, it's crucial to understand not just the current capabilities of AI, but also the trajectory of its development. Emerging AI technologies will redefine how creative professionals generate, refine, and optimize their work, reshaping industries from marketing to entertainment.

In this chapter, we will explore some of the most promising trends and tools in AI-powered content creation and look ahead to the future of AI in creative fields. With this knowledge, you'll be better equipped to navigate the evolving landscape and continue thriving in an AI-enhanced creative world.

Emerging AI Technologies in Creative Fields

AI has already proven its worth in content creation, but its future potential is vast. New advancements in machine learning, natural language processing, and neural networks are continually improving the capabilities of AI tools. Let's explore some of the most exciting AI technologies on the horizon that will change how content is created in writing, design, and music.

1. Advanced Natural Language Processing (NLP) and AI Writing Tools

AI-powered writing tools like **Jasper**, **Copy.ai**, and **Grammarly** have transformed the way writers approach content creation. However, the next wave of NLP advancements will enable even more sophisticated tools that can understand context, tone, and style at a deeper level.

- **Next-Gen GPT Models**: Future iterations of GPT models will become even more powerful, enabling more nuanced content generation. These advanced models will be able to create complex narratives, understand context across long-form content, and produce writing that's indistinguishable from human authors.

- **Real-Time Collaboration with AI**: AI will become an integral part of the collaborative writing process. Imagine an AI-powered co-writer that not only suggests improvements in real-time but also helps you brainstorm, generate ideas, and develop story arcs. This will lead to faster creation of high-quality content and more productive collaboration between humans and machines.

- **Personalized Content Creation**: With future advancements, AI writing tools will be able to create deeply personalized content for readers. Whether it's blog posts, product descriptions, or marketing emails, AI will generate content tailored to an individual's interests, preferences, and browsing behavior, taking content personalization to the next level.

Key Trends:

- Enhanced contextual understanding for more relevant and engaging writing.

- Real-time collaboration between AI and human writers.

- Increased personalization capabilities to improve reader engagement.

2. AI-Powered Design Tools: The Next Generation

Design has long been a domain where human creativity has reigned supreme. However, AI is now helping designers work smarter, not harder. With tools like **Canva**, **Adobe Sensei**, and **Crello**, AI is already assisting designers in generating layouts, color palettes, and image compositions. But as AI in design continues to evolve, the possibilities for automating and enhancing design processes will be even more powerful.

- **Generative Design**: AI tools will increasingly enable generative design, where algorithms can create entire visual compositions based on input criteria. Designers will be able to input a basic concept, and AI will generate multiple variations of a design, allowing for quicker ideation and exploration of different aesthetics.

- **Intuitive AI Design Assistants**: As AI's understanding of design principles improves, design assistants will become more intuitive and capable of making style suggestions based on context. These tools will help designers maintain brand consistency across all visual elements, suggesting design tweaks based on a company's existing assets.

- **Augmented Reality (AR) and AI-Driven Design**: AI tools will integrate with AR technology to create immersive, interactive designs. Designers will be able to use AI to create not just static images but dynamic, interactive visual content for everything from websites to video games.

Key Trends:

- Increased use of AI for generative design and rapid prototyping.

- AI-driven design assistants that adapt to individual stylistic preferences.

- Integration of AI with AR for next-gen interactive design experiences.

3. AI in Music: The Future of Sound Creation

The music industry has seen a surge of AI tools that assist in composition, mixing, and mastering. Platforms like **AIVA, Amper Music,** and **Soundraw** have revolutionized the process of music creation by enabling creators to generate original music with minimal effort. However, the future of AI in music creation promises even greater innovation.

- **AI-Driven Music Composition**: Future AI music tools will be capable of generating complex, multi-layered compositions in real time. These AI systems will adapt to a creator's unique style and collaborate to produce original music that reflects the artist's vision.

- **Emotionally Intelligent AI**: One of the most exciting advancements will be AI systems that can detect and create music based on emotions. These systems will analyze the emotional tone of a project—whether it's a video, game, or film—and generate a soundtrack that complements the mood. This could revolutionize how composers and sound designers work with AI to create more emotionally resonant pieces.

- **Real-Time Music Collaboration**: AI tools will allow musicians to collaborate with AI in real-time, creating music together. Whether it's through automated song structures, AI-generated beats, or assistance with chord progressions, musicians will have AI as a true creative partner, pushing the boundaries of traditional music composition.

Key Trends:

- Real-time AI-driven music composition and improvisation.

- Emotionally intelligent AI that creates music to match specific moods.

- AI-powered collaboration tools for musicians to co-create with artificial intelligence.

Trend Watch: The Latest AI Tools and Their Impact

AI tools are being developed at an incredible rate, and staying informed about the latest innovations will allow you to adapt quickly to the changing landscape. Below, we'll look at some of the cutting-edge AI tools that are already making waves in content creation.

1. DALL·E 2: Revolutionizing AI-Generated Art

DALL·E 2, an advanced image generation model developed by OpenAI, is a prime example of how AI is changing the world of visual arts. This AI tool can generate realistic images from textual descriptions, making it possible to create completely original artwork from simple prompts.

- **Impact on Design**: DALL·E 2 will allow designers to generate highly specific visuals on-demand, streamlining the creative process and opening up new possibilities for illustration, branding, and visual storytelling.

- **Future Possibilities**: As AI becomes more sophisticated, tools like DALL·E 2 will offer even more control over the details of the generated images. This will make it possible for creators to generate not only illustrations but highly tailored, contextual designs that match their specific vision.

2. Descript: AI-Powered Video Editing

Descript has revolutionized the video editing world with its AI-driven transcription and editing capabilities. Descript allows users to edit video by editing text, making it much easier to trim, reorder, or rewrite video content.

- **Impact on Content Creation**: Descript's AI-powered tools make video editing accessible to creators who may not have technical expertise in video production. By transcribing audio and enabling text-based editing, Descript has made it possible for creators to produce high-quality videos more efficiently.

- **Future Possibilities**: As Descript continues to develop, it will likely integrate more AI features, such as automated content summarization, enhanced editing suggestions, and AI-driven script writing, allowing creators to produce complex videos with minimal effort.

3. Runway: AI Video Editing for Creators

Runway is an AI-powered creative suite that provides a range of tools for video creators, including real-time video editing, background removal, and AI-driven object tracking. Runway's ability to perform complex tasks automatically is helping creators push the boundaries of what's possible in video production.

- **Impact on Video Production**: Runway's AI tools streamline the video editing process by automating many time-consuming tasks. This allows creators to focus on more creative aspects of video production, such as storytelling and visual effects.

- **Future Possibilities**: As Runway evolves, it will likely offer even more advanced tools, such as AI-driven special effects, automated scriptwriting, and real-time collaboration features that make video production more collaborative and intuitive.

Hands-On Activity: Trend Watch

To stay ahead of the curve, it's important to actively explore the latest AI tools and trends in content creation. In this hands-on activity, you will research new AI tools or trends and reflect on how they could improve your own creative process.

Step 1: Research New AI Tools and Trends

Use online resources such as tech blogs, AI research papers, and industry news outlets to find the latest AI tools and trends in your field of content creation. For example, you might look for:

- New AI music tools for composition and sound design.

- Emerging AI writing assistants with advanced contextual understanding.

- Innovative AI design platforms that help streamline visual content creation.

Step 2: Reflect on How These Tools Could Benefit Your Work

Consider how these new AI tools could improve your current creative process. Could a new AI writing tool help you generate better content faster? Could AI-driven design suggestions save you time in creating marketing materials? Could AI in music composition help you experiment with new sounds or genres?

Step 3: Experiment with a New Tool

Select one of the tools you researched and try it out in your own creative process. Use it to generate content, create a design, or produce music. Reflect on how the tool enhances your workflow and creative output.

Real-World Applications: Preparing for the Future of AI

To stay competitive in your creative field, it's essential to embrace the upcoming changes in AI. Here are some strategies for preparing for the future of AI in content creation:

1. Stay Informed About Emerging AI Tools

Make it a habit to follow industry trends, attend AI conferences, and engage with communities that discuss the future of AI in creative fields. By staying informed, you can quickly adapt to new tools and integrate them into your workflow.

2. Experiment with AI Tools Regularly

Don't wait for AI tools to become mainstream before you start experimenting with them. Regularly test out new AI tools and features to understand how they can enhance your creative work. This will ensure that you stay ahead of the competition and can incorporate the latest advancements into your projects.

3. Leverage AI for Creativity, Not Just Efficiency

AI tools can improve efficiency, but their true value lies in their ability to spark new ideas and expand your creative boundaries. Use AI to experiment with different ideas, explore new creative territories, and generate content that you might not have thought of on your own.

Conclusion

The future of AI in content creation is incredibly exciting. As AI technologies continue to evolve, they will offer new possibilities for writers, designers, musicians, and all types of creators to push their boundaries and explore uncharted creative territories. By staying informed about emerging AI trends, testing new tools, and integrating them thoughtfully into your workflow, you can ensure that you remain at the forefront of this dynamic and rapidly changing landscape.

Chapter 14: Getting Started with AI in Your Work

Summary

Artificial Intelligence has already made a significant impact on the world of creative work. From writing and design to music production, AI tools are helping creators work more efficiently, innovate, and achieve higher-quality results. But for those new to AI in their creative process, the idea of integrating such tools into your daily workflow can seem overwhelming. In this chapter, we'll break down practical steps to help you get started with AI in your creative work.

We will cover the essentials of AI tool integration, how to choose the right tools for your projects, and best practices for effectively incorporating AI into your routine. By the end of this chapter, you will have the knowledge and confidence to use AI tools in your daily tasks, whether you're writing content, designing visuals, composing music, or tackling any other creative challenge.

In addition to providing clear guidelines for adopting AI tools, we will also guide you through a hands-on activity where you will create your first AI-powered project. This real-world exercise will give you the practical experience you need to begin using AI tools to improve your work.

Learning Objectives

By the end of this chapter, you will:

1. **Understand Where to Begin When Adding AI to Your Workflow**:
   Learn how to integrate AI tools into your current creative processes, ensuring you start small and scale as needed.

2. **Start Integrating AI Tools into Your Regular Creative Tasks**:
   Gain practical knowledge on which tools are

most beneficial for your specific projects, and how to apply them to enhance your creativity.

3. **Create Your First AI-Powered Project**: Gain hands-on experience by starting a project using AI tools. Whether it's writing, design, or music, you'll see how AI can help you streamline and elevate your work.

Introduction: The Case for Integrating AI into Your Creative Work

AI tools are not just a passing trend—they're here to stay and are transforming how we work. In creative fields, AI is enabling professionals to automate tedious tasks, generate fresh ideas, and create high-quality work in record time. The real value of AI lies in its ability to assist with repetitive or time-consuming processes, giving creators the freedom to focus on more important, high-value aspects of their work.

Incorporating AI into your creative process doesn't mean abandoning your style or your expertise. Instead, it allows you to work smarter, be more productive, and push the boundaries of your creativity. Whether you're looking to generate ideas, automate mundane tasks, or refine your existing work, AI can be a powerful ally.

However, diving into AI-powered tools can be intimidating, especially if you've never worked with them before. This chapter will walk you through practical steps to start integrating AI into your workflow, whether you're a writer, designer, musician, or any other type of creative professional. We'll cover the basics of how AI tools work, where to begin, and how to incorporate them into your daily tasks, ensuring that you can improve your creative process without feeling overwhelmed.

How to Start Using AI Tools in Your Creative Workflow

The first step to integrating AI into your workflow is to understand how to choose the right tools for your projects. With so many AI tools available across different creative disciplines, it's crucial to identify which ones will be most beneficial for your work. Here are some tips for getting started:

1. Choose the Right AI Tools for Your Needs

Different creative disciplines have different AI tools that are specifically designed to streamline tasks and enhance workflows. Here's a quick breakdown:

- **For Writing**: AI-powered writing tools like **Jasper**, **Grammarly**, and **Copy.ai** are excellent for generating content, improving readability, and refining style. These tools are ideal for content creators, marketers, and copywriters who need to produce high-quality text quickly.

- **For Design**: Tools like **Canva**, **Crello**, and **Adobe Sensei** are designed to assist with graphic design tasks. They use AI to suggest layouts, color palettes, and fonts based on your project's goals, making it easier to create visually appealing content even if you don't have extensive design experience.

- **For Music**: AI tools like **Amper Music**, **AIVA**, and **Soundraw** are great for generating original music. They provide customizable options for composing tracks in various genres, making it easier for creators to quickly generate high-quality music for their projects.

When selecting tools, consider your goals for the project and choose AI tools that complement your creative process. Start with one or two tools, experiment with them, and gradually expand your AI toolkit as you become more comfortable with the technology.

2. Start Small and Scale

When you first begin integrating AI into your work, don't try to overhaul your entire creative process all at once. Start small by using AI for specific tasks, such as idea generation or content refinement. For example, if you're a writer, you might use **Jasper** to help with generating article outlines or social media posts. If you're a designer, start by using **Canva's AI design assistant** to suggest layouts for your projects.

Once you become comfortable with using AI for certain tasks, you can gradually expand its use to more complex elements of your projects, such as drafting full-length articles, creating marketing campaigns, or producing music tracks. The key is to start small, build confidence, and allow AI to grow as a natural part of your creative process.

3. Integrate AI into Your Routine

AI tools should become a seamless part of your creative routine. You don't need to dedicate extra time to learn how to use them—simply integrate them into your existing workflow. For example, if you write blog posts regularly, make AI-generated drafts part of your standard process, where you use **Jasper** or **Copy.ai** to create initial drafts and then refine them yourself.

The goal is to use AI as a tool to accelerate tasks you already do, helping you produce content faster and with more precision. As you become more familiar with the tools, you'll find new ways to incorporate them into other parts of your creative process, from planning to final revisions.

Hands-On Activity: Create Your First AI-Powered Project

Now that you understand the basics of how to get started with AI in your creative workflow, it's time to take action. This hands-on activity will guide you through the process of starting your first AI-powered project. Whether you're a writer, designer, or musician, you'll use AI tools to improve your process and create a unique piece of content.

Step 1: Choose Your Creative Task

Decide what kind of project you want to start. Here are some suggestions based on different creative fields:

- **Writing**: Start a blog post, article, or social media post. Use an AI tool like **Jasper** or **Copy.ai** to generate an outline or draft.

- **Design**: Create a social media graphic, logo, or advertisement using **Canva** or **Crello**. Experiment with AI-generated layouts and design suggestions.

- **Music**: Create a background track for a video or podcast using **Amper Music** or **Soundraw**. Use the AI to generate an initial melody or beat.

Step 2: Use AI Tools to Generate Content

Once you've selected your project, use the AI tools to assist in generating content. For writing, this could mean generating a first draft or outline. For design, you might use AI to create the initial layout or select colors and fonts. For music, start by generating a basic melody or rhythm that can serve as the foundation of your track.

Take note of how the AI tools enhance your workflow. Did they save you time? Were the generated results aligned with your goals? These observations will help you understand how AI can complement your creative process.

Step 3: Add Your Personal Touch

Once the AI has generated the initial content, it's time to personalize it. AI tools can give you a great starting point, but your creative expertise is what will elevate the project. Refine the content, adjust the design, or tweak the music to align with your personal style or brand.

This step is where you should add your unique input. For example, you might:

- Refine AI-generated text to match your voice and audience.

- Adjust colors, layouts, and elements in AI-generated designs to reflect your aesthetic.

- Modify AI-generated music by adding new instruments, adjusting the tempo, or refining the arrangement.

The goal is to use AI as a foundation and build upon it with your creativity.

Step 4: Evaluate Your Results

After completing your project, take a moment to evaluate the results. Did the AI tools improve your creative process? Did you feel that your personal touch was evident in the final product? How did the AI enhance the efficiency or quality of your work?

Reflecting on these questions will help you understand the value AI brings to your workflow and how to integrate it more effectively in the future.

Real-World Applications: Using AI to Create and Improve Your Work

AI tools are not just for tech enthusiasts—they can help creators in real, tangible ways. Here's how you can use AI to improve your content creation and stay competitive in your field.

1. Streamlining Your Workflow

AI tools can automate many of the repetitive tasks that often slow down creative work. For example, writers can use AI to generate first drafts, marketers can use AI to create ad copy, and designers can leverage AI to quickly generate visual concepts. By using AI to handle these tasks, you can spend more time on the creative aspects of your projects, leading to higher-quality work and faster turnaround times.

2. Experimenting with New Ideas and Techniques

AI can help spark new ideas that you may not have considered on your own. For instance, AI-driven music tools can generate melodies in genres you've never worked with, giving you the inspiration to experiment with new sounds. Similarly, AI-powered design tools can suggest color schemes, layouts, and typography combinations that you might not have considered. These suggestions can push you outside your creative comfort zone and help you develop more innovative content.

3. Enhancing Your Creativity and Personal Style

While AI can generate content, it's your unique creative vision that makes your work stand out. By integrating AI into your workflow, you can use it as a tool to enhance and refine your personal style. AI can help you work faster and more efficiently, leaving you with more time to focus on the elements of your project that are uniquely yours.

Conclusion

Getting started with AI in your work doesn't have to be a daunting task. By taking small, deliberate steps and selecting the right tools for your needs, you can integrate AI into your creative workflow and start reaping the benefits today. AI can help streamline your process, generate new ideas, and improve the quality of your work, all while allowing you to maintain your unique creative voice.

This chapter has provided you with the tools, tips, and hands-on experience to begin using AI in your projects. As you continue to explore AI's potential, you'll find that it's not just about automating tasks— it's about working smarter and unleashing new levels of creativity.

Chapter 15: Final Thoughts and Moving Forward with AI

Summary

As we come to the end of this journey into the world of AI-powered content creation, it's important to reflect on everything you've learned and how you can continue to use AI tools to enhance your creativity. The future of AI in creative fields is bright, and now you have the foundational knowledge to use these tools effectively in your daily work. Whether you're a writer, designer, musician, or entrepreneur, AI has the potential to streamline your process, spark new ideas, and help you create high-quality content faster than ever before.

In this final chapter, we'll recap the key takeaways from our exploration of AI tools, discuss how to keep improving and expanding your skills, and offer practical advice on how to continue your AI journey. By setting clear goals and maintaining an attitude of experimentation, you'll be well-equipped to integrate AI into your future projects and continue staying ahead in an AI-driven creative landscape.

Learning Objectives

By the end of this chapter, you will:

1. **Feel Confident Using AI for Various Creative Projects**:
   Gain a solid understanding of how to use AI tools in writing, design, music, and other creative fields, ensuring you feel comfortable incorporating them into your workflow.

2. **Learn How to Continue Learning and Experimenting with New AI Tools**:
   Understand the importance of continual learning and experimentation with AI, keeping up with new tools and trends to stay competitive in your creative career.

3. **Set Clear Goals for Using AI in Future Projects**:
   Create a plan for how to integrate AI into your next creative project and beyond, with a focus on setting goals, refining your process, and staying on top of industry advancements.

Introduction: A Reflection on Your AI Journey

Looking back at everything you've learned, it's clear that AI is not just a tool—it's a transformative force in the creative process. As AI technology evolves, so too does the potential for innovation in writing, design, music, and beyond. From automating repetitive tasks to generating new ideas and refining content, AI offers creators the opportunity to work more efficiently and push the boundaries of their imagination.

However, AI is not meant to replace human creativity. Rather, it serves as a powerful tool that can amplify your abilities, giving you more time to focus on high-value, creative aspects of your projects. By integrating AI into your workflow, you're positioning yourself at the forefront of the creative industry, and now you're equipped with the knowledge to continue exploring, experimenting, and improving.

As you move forward, remember that learning and experimentation are key. AI is a rapidly evolving field, and new tools and technologies are constantly emerging. By staying curious and open to new possibilities, you can ensure that your creative career remains dynamic and future-proof.

Recap of Key Learnings

Throughout this book, we've explored the various ways AI can support and enhance the creative process. Let's review the main takeaways that will serve as the foundation for your continued AI journey:

1. Understanding AI's Role in Content Creation

AI is a tool that can augment your creativity, not replace it. We've learned how AI-powered writing tools like **Jasper**, **Grammarly**, and **Copy.ai** can help streamline content generation, while design tools like **Canva**, **Crello**, and **Adobe Sensei** assist in creating high-quality visuals quickly. In music, AI-driven platforms like **Amper Music** and **AIVA** help creators generate original compositions, while maintaining a human touch in the creative process.

2. The Integration of AI Into Your Workflow

You've learned how to integrate AI into your existing workflow, whether you're writing, designing, or composing music. The key is to start small, use AI for specific tasks, and then gradually expand its use as you become more comfortable with the tools. This integration ensures that AI complements your creative process without taking over.

3. AI's Potential to Enhance Creativity

AI can help you generate new ideas, refine your existing content, and push the boundaries of what's possible. By using AI to automate repetitive tasks, you can focus on more creative aspects of your work, such as conceptualization, refinement, and personalization.

4. Hands-On Experience with AI Tools

You've had the opportunity to experiment with AI tools in real-world applications, from writing blog posts and designing graphics to composing music. These hands-on experiences have given you a deeper understanding of how AI works in practice and how you can tailor it to your own creative needs.

Moving Forward: Embracing AI as Part of Your Creative Process

As you continue your journey with AI, here are some practical strategies to help you stay on top of emerging trends and refine your use of AI tools in your creative work.

1. Keep Experimenting with New Tools

AI is a rapidly evolving field, and new tools are emerging every day. To stay ahead of the curve, make it a habit to explore new AI tools and incorporate them into your workflow. Whether it's a new AI writing assistant, design tool, or music composition platform, experimenting with these tools will give you a competitive edge and help you discover innovative ways to enhance your creative projects.

Consider setting aside regular time to explore new AI tools, testing them out on small projects before deciding whether to integrate them into your routine. Don't be afraid to fail or make mistakes during this process—it's all part of learning and growing.

2. Set Clear Goals for AI Integration

As you continue using AI in your work, set specific goals for how you want to integrate AI into future projects. Do you want to speed up your content creation process? Are you looking to enhance the quality of your designs? Or perhaps you want to explore new ways to experiment with music composition? Setting clear goals will help you focus on the areas where AI can have the most significant impact on your creative work.

For example, your goal could be to use AI tools to draft a full-length blog post in under an hour, or to create a unique music track using AI-generated melodies and then refining them with your personal style. Setting measurable goals will allow you to track your progress and see tangible improvements over time.

3. Stay Curious and Keep Learning

The world of AI is evolving quickly, with new tools and advancements being introduced regularly. Staying curious and continuously learning about the latest AI technologies is crucial to maintaining a competitive edge. Subscribe to industry blogs, attend AI-related webinars and conferences, and engage with communities that discuss the future of AI in creative fields.

By maintaining a mindset of continuous learning, you'll stay informed about emerging trends and be ready to incorporate the newest AI tools into your workflow. This will not only help you keep up with changes in the industry but also position you as a forward-thinking creative professional.

Hands-On Activity: Plan Your Next Steps

Now that you've reflected on your AI journey and learned how to integrate AI tools into your creative process, it's time to plan your next steps. This activity will help you set goals for using AI in your next creative project and ensure that you continue experimenting with new tools.

Step 1: Choose Your Next Project

Select a creative project that you will work on using AI tools. This could be anything from writing a blog post to creating a marketing campaign or producing a piece of music. Choose something that aligns with your goals for using AI and will allow you to experiment with the tools you've learned about in this book.

Step 2: Set Clear Goals

Set specific, measurable goals for the project. For example:

- **Writing**: "Use **Jasper** to generate an outline and first draft of my blog post in 30 minutes, then refine the content using my voice and style."

- **Design**: "Create a new social media ad using **Canva**'s AI design suggestions, then tweak the colors, layout, and typography to match my brand."

- **Music**: "Generate a melody using **Amper Music**, then add my own instruments and effects to produce a complete track."

By setting clear goals, you will have a roadmap for integrating AI into your work and a benchmark to evaluate how AI tools improve your creative process.

Step 3: Experiment with New AI Tools

As part of your project, consider experimenting with a new AI tool that you haven't used before. This will allow you to expand your skill set and explore different possibilities within your creative work.

For instance, if you've mostly used **Jasper** for writing, you might experiment with **Copy.ai** to generate a different style of content. If you've been working with **Canva**, try **Crello** to see how its design assistant features differ. For music, if you've used **Amper Music**, experiment with **Soundraw** to explore new genres and styles.

Step 4: Reflect on Your Progress

After completing your project, take time to reflect on how AI tools improved your creative process. Did they save time? Did they enhance your creativity? Did you learn something new about your workflow or the tools you used?

By reflecting on these questions, you'll gain valuable insights into how AI can be further integrated into your future projects and how you can continue optimizing your creative workflow.

Real-World Applications: Building Your Creative Career with AI Tools

AI tools are not only useful for improving your workflow—they are essential for building a sustainable, future-proof creative career. By continuing to experiment with AI, refining your skills, and staying ahead of industry trends, you can ensure that your career remains competitive in an AI-driven world. Here are some real-world applications of AI tools that will help you grow as a creative professional:

1. Enhance Your Productivity

AI tools can help you produce high-quality work faster, allowing you to take on more projects and clients. By automating time-consuming tasks like drafting content, designing visuals, or generating music, you can focus on the creative aspects that require your expertise. This not only increases your productivity but also enables you to deliver better results in less time.

2. Stay Ahead of Industry Trends

The creative industry is constantly evolving, and AI is one of the driving forces behind that change. By using

AI tools in your work, you demonstrate that you are adaptable and innovative. Whether you're working in design, writing, music, or any other creative field, staying ahead of AI trends will help you stay competitive and relevant.

3. Attract Clients and Opportunities

Clients and employers are increasingly looking for professionals who can leverage AI to create high-quality content efficiently. By showcasing your ability to work with AI tools, you can attract new clients, land better opportunities, and position yourself as a leader in your field.

Conclusion

As we conclude this journey into the world of AI in creative work, it's clear that AI is here to stay. By understanding how to integrate AI into your workflow and continuously experimenting with new tools, you can stay at the forefront of this rapidly evolving industry. Whether you're a writer, designer, musician, or entrepreneur, AI has the potential to enhance your creativity, streamline your work, and help you achieve better results in less time.

Your journey with AI is just beginning. By setting clear goals, experimenting with new tools, and staying curious, you can continue evolving your creative process and build a future-proof career that thrives in an AI-driven world. The possibilities are endless, and with AI by your side, you can continue pushing the boundaries of what's possible in content creation.